D1565182

EIGHT
BLACK
AMERICAN
INVENTORS

*For my wife Charlene
and our four children
Robbie, Debbie, Kevin, and Karen*

EIGHT BLACK AMERICAN INVENTORS

ROBERT C. HAYDEN

ADDISON-WESLEY

1972

 **An Addisonian Press Book**

Also by Robert C. Hayden

SEVEN BLACK AMERICAN SCIENTISTS

Addison-Wesley Publishing Company, Inc.
Reading, Massachusetts 01867

Library of Congress Catalog Card Number 78–164402
Printed in the United States of America
ISBN:0-201-02823-9

TABLE OF CONTENTS

INVENTIONS AND THE BLACK AMERICAN

Eli Whitney invented the cotton gin. True or False? Since 1792 most people have learned and believed this statement. American history books give him full credit for inventing a machine that could separate cotton fibers from seeds. For a person to prove that an invention is his alone, he or she must be awarded a patent from the United States Patent Office. A patent is a grant from the United States Government giving an inventor all rights to his invention. Even though Eli Whitney received a patent and full credit for the first cotton gin—*he may not have been the true inventor*. Instead, the real inventor could well have been a black slave who worked on a southern cotton plantation.

Whitney was a native of New England, who went south to study law and to be a teacher on a cotton plantation.

7

He noticed how difficult it was to separate the seeds from cotton by hand. This work was done by slaves and a slave could clean only a few pounds of cotton a day.

On one of his trips to Georgia, Whitney saw a crude comb-like instrument that loosened the seeds from cotton. It had been made and was being used by a slave. The slave, whose name was Sam as the story goes, had learned how to make this laborsaving tool from his father. Eli Whitney improved upon and perfected the slave's invention.

Up to this time, the United States shipped about 138,000 pounds of cotton to different parts of the world each year. Several years later, using the cotton gin, the United States exported over six million pounds a year.

Who was the real inventor of the cotton gin, a black man or a white man? This question can be asked about many inventions of the 1700's and 1800's. We will never know the whole truth about the cotton gin, or for that matter, about many inventions by black people. Their ideas were often stolen by their white masters.

Before the end of the Civil War (1865), noteworthy inventions by blacks were not numerous. For most slaves the foremost question was how to gain their freedom. Those with intelligence and vision used their minds to devise plans and to interest others in gaining freedom from slavery. Many free black people worked to save their black brothers. They did so by developing their literary and speaking ability rather than by becoming machinists, engineers or inventors.

During this same period most of the labor and mechanical industries of the South were carried on with slave labor. Bits and pieces of history show that many of the simple tools of the day were designed by slaves. They invented various pieces of equipment to lessen the burden of their daily work. None of these, however, could be patented by the United States Patent Office. Worthwhile ideas perfected by blacks, were forever lost because of the attitude of the Federal Government at the time.

In 1858, Jeremiah S. Black, Attorney General of the United States, had ruled that since a patent was a contract between the government and the inventor, and since a slave was not considered a United States citizen, he could neither make a contract with the government nor assign his invention to his master. Thus it has been impossible to prove the contributions of many unnamed slaves whose creative skill has added to the industrial growth of our country.

Jo Anderson, a slave on the plantation of Cyrus McCormick, is said to have made a major contribution to the McCormick Grain Harvester. Yet, he is only credited in the official records as being a handyman or helper to McCormick.

In 1862, a slave owned by Jefferson Davis, President of the Confederacy, invented a propeller for ocean vessels. With a model of his invention the slave showed remarkable mechanical skill in wood and metal working. He was unable to get a patent on his propeller, but the merits of his invention were reported in many Southern newspapers. The propeller was finally used in ships of the Confederate Navy.

The national ban on patents for slaves did not apply to those made by "free persons of color." So, when James Forten (1776–1842) perfected a new device for handling sails, he had no trouble getting one. From his invention he was able to earn a good living for himself and his family. This was also true of another black, Norbert Rillieux, whom you will read about later on.

It is believed that Henry Blair was the first black American to be granted a United States patent. He received his first patent in 1834 for a seed planter. In 1836, Blair received his second patent on a corn harvester. In both cases he was described in the official records as "a colored man."

Following the Civil War, the growth of industry in this country was tremendous. Much of this was made possible from the inventions of both blacks and whites. By 1913, an estimated one thousand inventions had been patented by black Americans in such fields as industrial machinery, rapid transportation, and electrical equipment.

Let's look at the inventions made by black people after the war when legal slavery ended and fewer obstacles stood in the way. Industrial opportunities were generally available to everyone. There was a freer market and the records prove that blacks had just as much inventive ability as whites. It is interesting to see how the inventions of black people have been recorded.

Since Blair received his second patent, the United States Patent Office has never kept a record of whether an inventor was black or white. However, on two different occasions the Patent Office has sought this information. The first inquiry was made in the year 1900 by the Patent Office for the United States Commission that was preparing an exhibit on black Americans for a fair in Paris. The second was made in 1913 at the request of the Pennsylvania Commission planning a freedom exhibit in Philadelphia. In both cases the Patent Office sent out several thousand letters to patent lawyers, large manufacturing firms, and to the various newspapers edited by black men. The people who received the letters were asked to inform the Commission of Patents of any patents granted by the office for inventions by black people. The letter sent out by the Patent Office in 1900 read as follows:

DEPARTMENT OF THE INTERIOR
United States Patent Office

Washington D.C., January 26, 1900

Dear Sir:

This Office is endeavoring to obtain information concerning patents issued to colored inventors, in accordance with a request from the United States Commission to the Paris Exposition of 1900, to be used in preparing the "Negro Exhibit."

To aid in this work, you are requested to send to this Office, in the enclosed envelope, which will not require a postage stamp, the names of any colored inventors you can furnish, together with the date of grant, title of invention, and patent number, so that a list without errors can be prepared.

You will confer a special favor by aiding in the preparation of this list by filling in the blank form below, and sending in any replies as promptly as possible. Should you be unable to furnish any data, will you kindly inform us of that fact?

Very respectfully,

O. H. Duell,
Commissioner of Patents

The replies were numerous. The information showed that a very large number of blacks had contacted lawyers. Even so, many were unable to get patents because they lacked the necessary funds to apply for them. Some had actually obtained them but the records of most lawyers were poorly kept and so the names and inventions of many blacks were lost.

Patents were often taken out in the name of the lawyer. A large number of black inventors allowed this because they felt that the racial identity of the inventor would lower the value of a patented invention. Yet more than a thousand patents were fully identified by the name of the inventor, date, patent number and title of invention as being owned by blacks. These patents represented inventions in nearly every branch of industrial arts such as household goods, mechanical appliances, electrical devices and chemical compounds. In the beginning, agricultural and home utensils were most common. But gradually the black inventor widened the field of his efforts. Here is just a small part of a list of black inventors in the United States. The entire record included nearly 190 inventors and 370 inventions. Some of the people received more than one patent.

Inventor	Invention	Date	Patent Number
Blair, H.	Corn Planter	10/14/1834	
Blair, H.	Corn Planter	8/31/1836	
Ashbourne, A. P.	Process for Preparing Cocoanut for Domestic Use	6/1/1875	163,962
Bailiff, C. O.	Shampoo Headrest	10/11/1898	612,008
Beard, A. J.	Car Coupler	11/23/1897	594,059
Becket, G. E.	Letter Box	10/4/1892	483,525
Bowman, H. A.	Making Flags	2/12/1892	469,395
Brooks, C. B.	Street Sweepers	3/17/1896	556,711
Burr, J. A.	Lawn Mower	5/9/1899	624,749
Butler, R. A.	Train Alarm	6/15/1897	584,540
Campbell, W. S.	Self-Setting Animal Trap	8/30/1881	246,369
Creamer, H.	Steam Traps	3/8/1888	358,964
Davis, W. D.	Riding Saddles	10/6/1896	568,969
Faulkner, H.	Ventilated Shoes	4/29/1890	426,495
Ferrell, F. J.	Valves for Steam Engine	5/27/1890	428,671
Grant, G. F	Golf Tee	12/12/1899	638,920
Headen, M.	Foot Power Hammer	10/5/1886	350,363
Johnson, W.	Eggbeater	2/5/1884	292,821
Latimer, L. H.	Manufacturing Carbons	6/17/1882	252,386
Lee, J.	Bread Crumbing Machine	6/4/1895	540,553
Matzeliger, J. E.	Shoe Lasting Machine	9/22/1891	459,899
McCoy, E.	Lubricator for Steam Engines	7/2/1872	129,843
(McCoy received 25 patents for different types of lubricators between 1872 and 1899.)			
Miles, A.	Elevator	10/11/1887	371,207
Murray, G. W.	Fertilizer Distributor	6/5/1894	520,889

Inventor	Invention	Date	Patent Number
Pickering, J. F.	Air Ship	2/20/1900	643,795
Purvis, W. B.	Paper Bag Machine	1/28/1890	420,099
Sampson, G. T.	Clothes Drier	6/7/1892	476,416
Smith, P. D.	Potato Digger	1/21/1891	445,206
White, J. T.	Lemon Squeezer	12/8/1896	572,849
Winters, J. R.	Fire Escape Ladder	5/7/1878	203,517
Woods, G. T.	Railway Telegraph	11/15/1887	373,383

The most significant black inventors following the Civil War were Elijah McCoy, Jan Matzeliger, Granville T. Woods, Lewis H. Latimer and Garrett A. Morgan. McCoy who held more than fifty patents, was born to slave parents who escaped to Canada. His greatest contribution was the lubricating cup that fed oil to machinery while it was still running. Jan E. Matzeliger developed machinery that radically changed the manufacturing of shoes in this country. Unable to sell his invention himself, Matzeliger sold his rights to the United Shoe Machinery Company, which developed into the United Shoe Machinery Corporation. Lewis Latimer worked with Alexander Graham Bell and Thomas Edison. He wrote a book explaining Edison's electric light and served as Edison's star witness in many patent cases. Garrett A. Morgan invented a gas mask used in World War I and later an automatic traffic light that brought safety to people traveling on streets and highways.

In addition to the lives and works of these men, several others, are presented in this book. Two of them, Lewis

Temple and Norbert Rillieux lived before the Civil War. Temple invented a harpoon that brought sweeping changes to the whaling industry. Rillieux's invention revolutionized the processing of sugar. One inventor you will read about lived in more recent years. Frederick Jones, who died in 1961, invented a refrigeration unit that made possible the truck transportation of frozen and perishable foods that must be kept cold until they reach the supermarket shelves. And the last inventor you will read about, Granville T. Woods, sometimes called the "Black Edison," held over 35 patents on electrical devices sold to American Bell Telephone, General Electric, and Westinghouse Air Brake.

GARRETT A. MORGAN

1877–1963

His Inventions Saved Lives

On July, 25, 1916, a violent explosion ripped through Tunnel No. 5 of the Cleveland Waterworks. The tunnel was 250 feet below the surface of Lake Erie. At the moment of the explosion more than 30 men were working there. Deadly gases, heavy smoke, dust, and debris quickly filled the underground space. The men were trapped inside.

Firemen, doctors, nurses, policemen, and waterworks employees gathered at the tunnel's entrance. Relatives and friends of the trapped men stood by grimly. No one knew the fate of the trapped workers. Staying alive for more than a few hours wasn't likely. Someone would have to enter the tunnel if the men were to be found and carried out. But the heavy smoke and poisonous gases made it impossible for anyone to try. Chances of rescuing the workers seemed hopeless.

In the city of Cleveland, Garrett A. Morgan was resting at his home. Someone at the scene of the tunnel explosion remembered that recently a black man had been demonstrating a gas inhalator, trying to interest manufacturers in his invention. He had received a patent for this invention four years earlier and had been awarded First Grand Prize for his gas inhalator at an international safety and sanitation exposition in New York City. But, he had not been too successful in selling his invention.

But now someone contacted Morgan and asked him to come to the tunnel immediately, with several of his gas inhalators. Morgan arrived at the Lake Erie tunnel with his brother. Quickly they and two other volunteers donned Morgan's gas mask and descended into the tunnel in search of the trapped men. They were the only ones able to enter the smoke and gas-filled tunnel and reach the bodies of the unconscious and dead men. The gas inhalators allowed them to breathe clean air carried in a pouch of the inhalator. Garrett Morgan led the rescue team in and out of the tunnel many times. Together they saved the lives of 32 people by carrying them out of the tunnel to the waiting crowd.

This heroic act thrust Morgan before the public. Suddenly manufacturers and fire departments across the country became interested in his gas inhalator, or gas mask as we would call it today. Orders for the mask poured into Cleveland from fire companies all over the United States. And, Morgan was asked to talk about and demonstrate his invention in many cities and towns. He was awarded a solid gold diamond studded medal by the City of Cleveland for his courage. But more important, his heroism also helped to prove the value of his invention.

However, when it became known that Garrett Morgan was a black man, many orders for his gas mask were cancelled. When he traveled in the South it was necessary for him to have a white man demonstrate his invention while he passed himself off as an Indian.

Garrett Morgan was not discouraged by the discrimination he faced as a black American inventor, and he continued to perfect his first gas mask. During World War I American soldiers used Morgan's improved mask in battle to protect them from deadly chlorine fumes. Morgan's invention saved many lives.

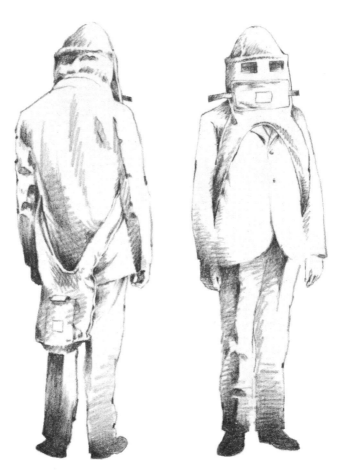

Morgan's safety helmet was designed for speedy work. It could be put on in seven seconds and taken off in three. Clean air was supplied from a bag of air suspended in the rear by two tubes leading from the hood. There was enough air in the bag to permit a man to stay in the midst of suffocating gases and smoke from 15 to 20 minutes. The helmet was especially designed to work in heavy smoke and among chemicals that produced dangerous or offensive fumes.

MORGAN'S NATIONAL SAFETY HOOD

Garrett Morgan received his first patent on a Safety Hood and Smoke Protector in 1912. During 1913 and 1914, Morgan's Style One Helmet, as it was called, passed many practical and rigid tests successfully. It met the approval of many fire chiefs in the United States and Canada. An article that appeared in the *New Orleans Times-Picyayune* on October 22, 1914, read as follows:

ABOUT MORGAN'S NATIONAL SAFETY HOOD AND SMOKE PROTECTOR

Spectacular Exhibit

One of the spectacular shows of the day was given by the National Safety Device Company with a Morgan Helmet. A canvas tent, close flapped and secure, was erected on an open space and inside the tent a fire started. The fuel was made up of tar, sulfur, formaldehyde, and manure, and the character of the smoke was the thickest and most evil smelling imaginable. Charles P. Salan, former director of public works of Cleveland under Mayor Johnson, conducted the tests. Fitting a big canvas affair that had the appearance of a diver's helmet on the head of "Big Chief" Mason, a full-blooded Indian, Mr. Salan sent the Indian under the flaps into the smoke-filled tent. The smoke was thick enough to strangle an elephant, but Mason lingered around in the suffocating atmosphere for a full twenty minutes and experienced no inconvenience. He came out after the test "as good as new," and a little later gave another exhibition. The Morgan Helmet is fitted with a long hose that reaches to the ground, where there is always the current of fresh air, no matter the thickness of the smoke.

In competitive tests, the Morgan Safety Smoke Hood easily proved itself superior. In proof, here is what Fire Chief J. J. Mulcahey, of Yonkers, New York, said:

"In a competitive test made at our headquarters, Saturday, September 15, 1914, between another make and the Morgan National Safety Helmet. The "other make" demonstrator remained in a gas and smoke filled room for fourteen minutes and the Morgan demonstrator remained in the same room for twenty-five minutes and when he came out he did not seem to be at all uncomfortable. We tried them both and we all prefer the Morgan Helmet, and I immediately placed an order for six Morgan Helmets upon the merits of the helmet and its demonstration, at a price of twenty-five dollars each, for general use in our department."

Fire Chief J. T. Mertz, of Akron, Ohio, had this to say:

"What is the use of fighting fires all night when you can stop them in minutes? Two men with a Morgan Smoke Hood and a good fire extinguisher can do more in the first fifteen minutes than a whole company can in the next half hour."

FROM SEWING MACHINES
TO HAIR STRAIGHTENING

Garrett Morgan was born on March 4, 1877, in Paris, Kentucky. His mother had been a slave who was freed by Lincoln's Emancipation Proclamation in 1863. He grew up on a farm with his brothers and sisters and was able to attend school through grade six.

When Morgan was fourteen years old he left home and traveled to Cincinnati to look for a job. Here he worked for four years as a general handyman for a wealthy landowner. During this time he hired a tutor to help him with his English grammar. In 1895, Morgan moved to Cleveland, Ohio, which was to be his home for the rest of his life.

His first job in Cleveland was that of a sewing machine adjuster for a clothing manufacturer. He loved to tinker with machinery and his skill at fixing mechanical things provided him jobs with several different firms.

In 1907, Morgan decided to start a business for himself and he opened a shop for repairing and selling sewing machines. He was a smart businessman and two years later he opened his own tailoring shop. He hired 32 workers and began making coats, suits, and dresses with the various sewing devices he had built himself.

One day, just before suppertime, Morgan was experimenting at home with a liquid that would give a high polish to sewing machine needles. A good polish would prevent a needle from scorching woolen material as it stitched. When Mrs. Morgan called her husband to the dinner table he hastily wiped the polishing liquid that was on his hands on a piece of wiry pony fur cloth lying on his workbench. When he returned from the dinner table, Morgan noticed that the wiry fuzz of the cloth where he had wiped his hands was quite straight.

Being naturally curious, Morgan began to think about what had happened to the fuzz of the cloth. His next door neighbor had an Airedale dog and Morgan begged his neighbor to let him try some of his needle polish on the dog's fur. The same thing happened—the dog's hair became so straight that the neighbor hardly recognized his pet.

Next Morgan tried the fluid on his own hair—applying a little bit at first—then gradually to all of his hair. The result was the same. Garrett Morgan had discovered, by chance, a process for straightening hair. He changed his "magic" liquid into a cream and organized the G.A.

Garrett Morgan successfully introduces his new hair refining company to the public.

Morgan Hair Refining Company to introduce his hair straightening process to the public. He also marketed a black hair oil stain for men whose hair was turning gray and a curved-tooth iron comb that he invented in 1910 for straightening women's hair.

Morgan's business enterprise prospered. He was able to buy his own home and an automobile. It is reported that he was the first black person in Cleveland to own a car. Undoubtedly, his experience in driving through the streets of Cleveland led him to another invention. One which is still with us today, on the street corners and highways across our country—the traffic light.

THE FIRST AUTOMATED
THREE-WAY TRAFFIC LIGHT

Garrett Morgan was a man who was always experimenting with new ideas. On November 20, 1923, his tinkering paid off when he was awarded a patent for inventing a three-way traffic signal.

The "Go-Stop" signals in general use before Morgan's invention were not practical because there was no neutral position. In other words, the signal indicated either stop or go. There was no yellow light signal as we know it today. Without a traffic officer present, the signals could be ignored completely. Morgan's traffic signal was designed so that the stop and go signs could be left in a position that enabled traffic to move in all directions even without an officer.

Morgan's idea also solved another problem. The traffic officer often failed to change the signal promptly. This occurred when he became tired and the delays usually confused both the drivers and the pedestrians.

When Morgan's signal was at the half-mast position as is shown in Figure 1 on the following page, cars using caution could move in all directions—north, south, east, and west, even when a traffic officer was not present. The half-mast position was used at night to mark dangerous intersections. When a driver approached Morgan's signal in the half-mast position he would do the same that today's driver would do when approaching a blinking yellow light—slow down and proceed with caution.

Figure 2 shows traffic moving east and west while the north and south traffic would be at a standstill. To stop

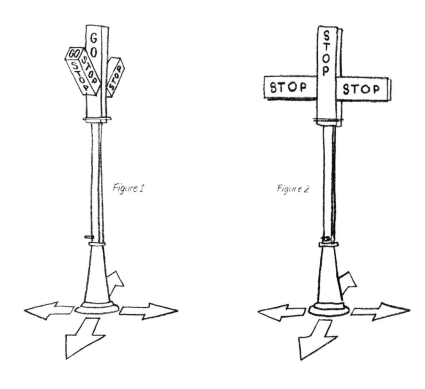

Figure 1

Figure 2

the east and west moving traffic, the signal post was rotated so that "Go" faced north and south as shown in Figure 3. Figure 4 shows the position of the signal that stopped traffic in all directions to allow pedestrians to cross the street in safety.

Today's traffic light signals makes orderly movement of vehicles possible on our highways and streets. It also provides for the safety of pedestrians crossing at busy intersections. In a simpler way, Morgan's signal did the same thing. He sold the rights to his invention to the

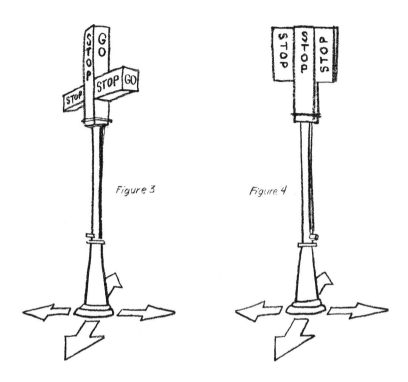

Figure 3

Figure 4

General Electric Corporation for $40,000 and it became the forerunner of the overhead and sidewalk lights that you see every day.

INVENTOR FOR SAFETY

It would be difficult to estimate how many lives have been saved because of Morgan's inventions. Many veterans of World War I certainly owed their lives to the gas mask they wore on the battlefield. The electric light signal system used in this country has been responsible for protecting human lives on our streets, highways and railways.

Morgan received several medals and citations for his inventions. The National Safety Device Co. awarded him a First Grand Prize for his gas inhalator. The United States government gave him a citation for his traffic signal device. The International Association of Fire Chiefs awarded him a gold medal and made him an honorary member.

In 1943, Morgan contracted glaucoma (an eye disease) which gradually made him almost blind during the latter years of his life. Each year until 1959, he traveled alone by train to the Mayo Clinic in Rochester, New York, for treatment of his eye condition. When Morgan died in 1963, he was given national recognition at the Emancipation Centennial Celebration held in Chicago. Five months after Garrett Morgan's death his granddaughter, Karen Morgan, wrote a biographical sketch on her famous grandfather. She recalled his life in this way:

"... coming from a poor family, G. A. Morgan did all he could to enrich both his life and that of his family. He was a jolly man, although he had his stern moments, and was very quick tempered and outspoken ... he gained some foes, but he had many friends, some of those being Mr. John D. Rockefellar, J. P. Morgan, ex-governor DiSalle, ex-mayor Cellebrezzi ... and other national, state, and local dignitaries. ...

Mr. Morgan was a down-to-earth practical man. He worked hard for everything he ever did or accomplished ... He was a lover of the great outdoors, of nature itself ... After he lost 90% of his sight he made constant use of his mind and his hands. He always kept himself busy. ...

With all of his achievements, recognition, and possessions, one fact remained to be true until his last breath . . . he was a plain man . . . proud to be an American, proud of his race.

His last goal or ambition in life was to be able to attend the Emancipation Centennial which was to be held in Chicago, in August of 1963. His wish was not fulfilled however, as he died one month before it was to take place. . . ."

LEWIS TEMPLE

1800–1854

To Catch a Whale

"August 2, 1761. Latitude 45° 54′ N., longitude 53° 37′ W., saw sperm-whale; killed one (sperm-whale is the male whale).

"August 6. Spoke to John Clasberry; he had got one hundred and five barrels; told us Seth Folger had got one hundred and fifty barrels. Spoke with two Nantucket men; they had got one whale between them; they told us that Jenkens and Dunham had got four whales, and Allen and Pease had got two whales between them. Latitude 42° 57′ N.

"August 28. Saw spermaceti, but could not strike. Latitude 43°.

"August 30. Saw spermaceti; foggy; lost sight of him.

"August 31. Saw spermaceti plenty; squally, and thunder.

"September 2. Saw spermaceti; foggy and dark.

"September 3. This morning at eight saw a spermaceti; got into her two short warps and the tow iron, but she ran away. In the afternoon came across her again; got another iron in, but she went away.

"September 5. Saw spermaceti; chased, but could not strike.

"September 6. Saw whales; struck one, but never saw her again.

"September 7. Saw small school of spermaceti. Captain Shearman struck one out of the vessel, and killed her. Latitude 43°."

During the days of American whaling, whalemen kept a diary of each voyage. The accounts above were taken from a page in an old whaler's logbook. There were many

reports like these. Probably the most valuable and interesting records of the old whaling days are found in the
logbooks kept by captains. Their voyages were long,
tedious, and dangerous. Some lasted as long as four
years.

Wooden block stamps were used for recording the
number of whales sighted and captured. When a whale
was captured the logbook page was stamped with a figure
that looked like this ⬛. A half whale that looked
like this ◤, meant that the whale got away. If you
were to look through the pages of a logbook from a whaling voyage, you would probably count more half whales
than whole whales and you would begin to realize that
although many whales were seen, few were caught. For
the methods of capture were far from being perfect.

To capture and kill a whale two basic weapons were
used—a harpoon and a lance. The job of the harpoon
was not to kill, but to first hook the whale, as a fishhook
does a fish. The long, spear-like lance was the killing
weapon. Only on rare occasions did the harpoon kill the
whale.

When a whaleboat was near its prey, the harpooner
would dart his weapon into its blubber. Attached to the
harpoon was some 1300 feet of rope. Once the whale was
"struck" the rope was tied to the boat.

The harpooned whale would dive down into the water
and dash off at a tremendous speed towing the boat with
its crew aboard. Sometimes the tow-line would be attached to a heavy wooden drag that the whale pulled through
the water as it tried to escape. Eventually, the whale

would tire from pulling the load and once again the whaleboat could approach the animal. The lance would then be thrown like a spear hoping to hit the lungs of the whale to kill it.

Many times, however, the lancer would not get a chance to throw his weapon. Often the pointed, barbed head of the harpoon was no match for the tremendous strength of the whale as it dove and twisted through the water, dragging the boat. The strength of a whale was so great that many harpoons were often twisted into fantastic shapes or broken. Frequently the whale pulled free from the hooked head of the harpoon and escaped. Sometimes the harpoon simply slipped out of the hole it had made in the whale's fleshy blubber. Too many whales were lost in this fashion.

In 1848, Lewis Temple, a black man in New Bedford, Massachusetts, invented a new type of harpoon. It had a movable head and worked in such a way as to prevent a harpooned whale from slipping loose from the hook and escaping. In Temple's harpoon the head became "locked" in the whale's flesh, and the only way to free it was to cut it loose after the whale was killed.

Catching whales was an ancient European industry, dating as far back as the 12th and 13th centuries. It was brought to the New England Colonies by some of its earliest settlers. The exact date whaling began in the New Bedford, Massachusetts area is uncertain, but it was at least as early as 1746.

During the 1800's, New Bedford was the capital of the whaling industry in America. The products that came

from whales—oil, meat, and whalebone—were important to the country's economy. In 1846, more than 700
whaling vessels sailed from some 23 ports located from
Maine to New Jersey. Many of these ports gave up whaling after 1847, but the fleets from New Bedford continued to grow. Whaling reached its peak in this area in
1857, with 329 whaleships employing about 10,000 men
from New Bedford and nearby towns. Temple's toggle
became the standard harpoon of the whaling industry.

It was not until Lewis Temple invented what became
known as the Toggle-Iron and later Temple's Iron, that
any real change was made in the method of catching
whales. In 1820, an authority on whaling wrote—"many
ingenious persons had tried to improve the whaling harpoon; and although various changes had been devised,
they had all given place to the simplicity of the ancient
harpoon." After Temple invented his first toggle harpoon it became the accepted whaling weapon. It was
made into more complex harpoons, such as those shot by
a gun, but was never improved upon in any basic way. In
1926, Clifford Ashley, an authority on whaling wrote—
"It is safe to say that the 'Temple-Toggle' was the most
important single invention in the whole history of whaling. It resulted in the capture of a far greater proportion
of the whales that were struck than had before been
possible."

Who was this black American whose invention changed American whaling, which in turn helped this country
to prosper? He was not a whaleman. He never went to
sea. Some say that he never learned to write his name.

TEMPLE—THE BLACKSMITH

Outfitting whaleships for a year or two of whale hunting was a huge and serious undertaking. It required the skills and work of many trades people, and during the 1800's many individuals in New Bedford were involved in it. There were sail makers, rope makers, oil barrel makers, oar makers, boat builders, and blacksmiths who hammered out whaling tools and weapons from hot iron and steel. Lewis Temple was one of these blacksmiths.

He was born in Richmond, Virginia in the year 1800. Whether he was a free man or a slave in the South during his childhood and youth is not known. How he happened to land in New Bedford around 1830 is not certain either, but during the 1800's it was one of the northern cities to which runaway slaves escaped. It was also one of the "stations" along the route of the famous Underground Railroad to Canada where many black people found freedom. The Underground Railroad was a network of homes and farms where antislavery people would hide escaping slaves and help them. Perhaps Temple was one of the more than 100,000 slaves who found their way to freedom via the Underground Railroad between 1810 and 1850. Perhaps he was already free and just decided to settle in New Bedford. In either case, in the late 1820's he was one of 315,000 free black people in the United States who were becoming successful.

By 1836, Temple was a well-known citizen in the village of New Bedford. He was married, had three children, and was working as a blacksmith. How he learned the metalwork trade is impossible to say.

By 1845, it seems that Temple was doing extremely well in the blacksmith business for he was able to build his own shop. The whaling business was booming at this time, and the manufacture of whaling products had become the leading industry in Massachusetts after shoes and textiles.

Undoubtedly Temple knew and talked with whalers who came to his blacksmith shop to have harpoons and other whaling tools made. From his conversations he learned about adventures at sea and the business of catching whales. He would probably also have learned that many whales escaped because the harpoon would not hold the whale. Complaints about the old-style harpoon were increasing. The urgent need for a new and better harpoon was apparent to many people. Temple clearly recognized the problem and worked quietly away in his shop on a new type of harpoon—one that would not pull out of the whale's blubber when the whale pulled and tugged with great force on the tow line.

His solution was the toggle harpoon. What was a toggle harpoon and how did it work? How was it different from the harpoons that had been used before?

TEMPLE'S TOGGLE IRON

A whaling harpoon can be thought of as having two parts —a *head* and a *shank*. Its length, from the the tip of its pointed head to the end of the shank, was about 33 inches. The steel head was welded to a tough iron shank. The end of the shank was attached to the end of a wooden pole about six feet in length. The whale line (rope) was tied to the end of the shank where it joined the wooden handle.

The head was shaped with a hook or barb that was supposed to hold the whale. The barb, or flue, as it was sometimes called, curved backward from the point of the harpoon head. (To get a good idea of what a flue is, look at the end of a fish hook.) Both single-flue and double-flue harpoons were used by American whalers. These two types of harpoons were handed down from the Dutch and English who whaled during the 1600's. They were the best that American whalers had to work with for many years.

It is important to note that the flued head was fixed or immovable. This is where Lewis Temple made his big change. He made the barbed head movable. The head of his harpoon was mounted on the shank so that it turned

American harpoon heads used in whaling from its ancient beginning through Lewis Temple's era. From left to right: double barb, single barb, Temple iron, improved Temple iron.

after piercing the flesh of the whale. It turned or *toggled* at a right angle to the shank. This prevented the harpoon from being drawn out when the struck whale moved away. Let's look at this toggle principle by another example.

Suppose you had a coat with wooden peg buttons. If you simply pushed the peg-shaped buttons through the button holes they wouldn't hold your coat very well. But if you turned each peg after pushing it through the eye-like slit, so that it turned at a right angle crossing the slit, then it would hold fast and not slip back through the hole. Temple used this same principle in the design of his harpoon.

When Temple's Toggle Iron entered the whale the barb was parallel with the shank. To hold the barbed head parallel until it had cut through the blubber, a wooden pin the size of a matchstick was used. It was placed in a hole that ran through the shank and the barb of the harpoon. Under the pull of the whale in its desperate attempt to escape, the wooden pin holding the barbed head in a fixed position was broken. This allowed it to toggle or turn across the end of the shank and become firmly anchored. The head in this position was not likely to slip out of the blubber and was more secure than in any other form of harpoon.

It was difficult for a time to get whalemen to use Temple's novel tool. But after a little experience, most whaling captains were convinced that Temple's Toggle Iron was far superior to the ordinary barbed type and was adopted by most American whalers.

Temple's harpoon was a simple device. As a matter of fact the toggle idea in harpoons did not originate with him. And, it is a wonder that it had not been used by American whalers before 1848. It has had a strange history of appearance, disappearance, and reappearance in whaling. Archaeologists have since discovered that prehistoric man in northern Eurasia used a type of toggle harpoon. Yet in the Middle Ages whalemen lost or forgot the toggle method. It seems that Europeans during this period used harpoons even more primitive than those used by the advanced stone age whalers of Norway. Only in the remote regions of the Arctic and along the northerly coasts of the Pacific Ocean was the toggle harpoon continuously used. It was even used by the Eskimos. For it enabled them to catch the sea animals that supplied them with their meat. West Greenland Eskimos were using a type of toggle harpoon in the 1600's. The toggle head of the Eskimos' harpoons was made from bone and was detachable. It pulled off the shank and worked into the blubber as the whale pulled on the tow line. During the 17th and 18th centuries, European whalers, mainly the Dutch and English, had a chance to observe the whaling tools of these Eskimos. Why they never adopted the Eskimos' toggle is hard to figure out.

About ten years before Temple's invention, some American whalemen had an opportunity to learn about the toggle harpoon. In 1835, a whaler discovered new whaling grounds near Alaska. This opened up more water for thousands of whaleships during the next ten years. In their trips to Alaska, the Americans met the

Eskimos and Pacific Coast Indians who were using a removable head toggle iron.

Some new experimental harpoons were tried and patented shortly before Temple's invention. These harpoons were exactly like the single-flue harpoons except that the diameter of the shank just in back of the head was much smaller than the rest of it. Instead of breaking off, it would bend inside the blubber. This bending, caused by the twisting of the whale as it tried to escape, produced a crude type of toggle.

Perhaps if Temple had not invented the toggle harpoon, the single-flue harpoon would have remained the favorite weapon of American whale fishery. And, whalemen would have had to take their chances at killing the whale if they were lucky enough not to lose it.

TEMPLE'S RISE AND FALL

Temple's invention encouraged others to develop new harpoons. During the second half of the 1800's over 100 different patents on harpoons were issued by the United States Patent Office in Washington. Most of them however, were basically the same as Temple's original model. Even the harpoons that were shot from a gun rather than those thrown by hand had the basic toggle head. Only one minor change was ever made in the original Temple iron. Macy, another blacksmith in New Bedford, manufactured a harpoon so that the head swung outside or over the shank. Temple's toggle head swung inside the shank, the shank being forked over it. Macy's change just made the toggle harpoon easier to manufacture.

For some reason unknown to us, Lewis Temple never patented his invention. Other blacksmiths were quick to copy the Temple-toggle. One whalecraft maker in New Bedford made 30,000 toggle harpoons between 1848 and 1868. And there were some eight or more blacksmith shops in New Bedford during this time.

After 1848, the pages of whaling logbooks began to take on a new look. The half-whale figures that were stamped on the pages to indicate that a whale had escaped did not appear as often. More full whale figures appeared in the daily reports of whaling captains. In trip after trip, the Temple iron was proving what it could do. In 1853, the whaleship *Ohio* returned home from the Arctic with 2,300 barrels of oil. In killing 21 bowhead whales only 8 harpoons were used. All of them were Temple irons.

Around 1852, Temple was making a fairly good living from the sale of his harpoons. But it was nowhere near the fortune he could have made if he had patented his invention. He was, however, able to buy the building next to his home and to set up a new blacksmith shop. His business continued to grow and he was becoming even more successful. In 1854, a construction firm was hired to build Temple a new and bigger shop out of brick. This shop was never finished. One night, during the Fall of 1853, Temple was walking near the site where his new shop was to be built. He stumbled over a board that was hidden by the darkness. The injuries he received were serious and prevented him from working. Unable to work, money became a problem. In May, 1854, Lewis Temple died of the injuries from his fall at the age of 54.

Although the City of New Bedford voted to pay Temple $2,000 for the injury and the time lost from his work, the money was never paid. Temple died a poor man. When his estate was settled, there was practically no money left for his wife and children. His home, blacksmith shop and its equipment, and the half-finished brick shop were used to pay his debts.

The only thing left was Temple's name and the harpoon that he invented. But in the years following his death, it was proven beyond doubt that his harpoon had revolutionized the whaling industry.

FREDERICK McKINLEY JONES

1893–1961

Keeping Things Cool

On a hot summer night in 1937, Frederick McKinley Jones was trying to cool off by driving around a lake in Minneapolis. He stopped his car to catch a breath of fresh air. The cool breeze coming off the lake was a relief from the sweltering heat in the city. But with his car windows down, mosquitoes swarmed in on him, and he was forced to close them. Then the heat inside the car became unbearable and so Fred Jones left the lakeside and headed home. As he drove along the highway, he asked himself why someone had not invented a device to air-condition a car.

The next morning Jones arrived early at the public library in Minneapolis. He located all the books he could find on refrigeration and air conditioning. Finding no evidence that anyone had ever developed an air conditioner for an automobile, Jones began to sketch a design for one. A week later he showed his plans for a car air conditioner to his boss, Mr. J. A. Numero. Mr. Numero was not impressed.

"It would be too heavy," he told Jones. "Also, it would be too expensive to make, and I don't think anyone would buy it. Besides, we're in the business of making equipment for theaters, so let's stick to that."

Fred Jones put his plans for a car air cooler aside. But the idea stayed in his mind and he kept on thinking about it and continued to read all he could find on the science of refrigeration and air cooling.

About a year later Mr. Numero was playing golf on a hot midsummer day with two friends. One friend was in the trucking business and the other was in the air conditioning business. Mr. Werner, the owner of the Werner Transportation Co., had lost a truckload of poultry when the ice blocks for keeping the poultry cold in the truck had melted before reaching the market. This was not the first time that he had lost a shipment of food and he shared his disgust with his golfing companions. It seemed quite surprising to him that someone had invented an air conditioner to cool buildings.

"Why can't someone make a machine that will keep the inside of a truck cool? It seems to me that if a movie theater can be cooled off then surely someone ought to be able to cool a truckload of chickens without having to use ice."

The air conditioning expert explained that so far attempts to do this had failed. The jarring and jolting of a truck on the highway made it impossible for a mechanical refrigerator to work properly.

As Numero drove his ball off the fourth tee he turned to Werner and told him jokingly—"I'll build you a refrigerator for your truck."

This was quite a boast for Mr. Numero who was in the business of manufacturing motion picture equipment. The threesome walked off the tee onto the fairway and the conversation turned back to golf. Little did Mr. Numero realize that the trucker had taken his remark seriously. And neither had he remembered Jones' idea for a car air-cooler.

A few weeks later Werner called Numero to tell him that he had purchased a new truck and was ready for Numero to work on a cooling unit for it. The same day a shining new aluminium van appeared in the parking lot of Numero's firm—Cinema Supplies, Inc. Mr. Numero was dumbfounded.

He called his friend Werner back on the phone—"I was just fooling around, really, just kidding, when I said I could build a refrigerator for your truck."

Fred Jones, an engineer at Numero's firm, had noticed the truck when it pulled into the parking lot and overheard the telephone conversation that his boss was having with Werner. Numero, who knew only about making sound equipment for movie theatres, was stuck with a truck in which he was supposed to install an air conditioning unit.

Jones saw that his boss was embarrassed and upset. He went out, climbed into the truck and took some measurements. He then worked throughout most of the night making calculations. The next day Jones told his boss that he could build the kind of air cooling unit that Mr. Werner wanted.

Jones knew that the earlier truck refrigerations units had been jolted into pieces. They had been "such big clunks" as he described them, and they took up too much space inside the truck itself. Jones had had much experience in building shock proof and vibration proof gadgets. After much figuring he came up with a light, compact, and sturdy unit that he thought would do the job. He installed this unit under the truck but it quickly broke down as it became mud clogged. So he mounted another similar unit to the forehead of the truck above the cab, where it would be out of the way and could use space that had been wasted. It worked.

Jones standing in front of an air-conditioned Werner Truck.

This invention led to the formation of a new firm by Numero and Jones. Their company began to manufacture a compact, automatic shock-proof air conditioner for truck transportation of foods. Today, this firm is a thriving company called Thermo King, located in Minneapolis, Minnesota. And Mr. J. A. Numero is still a very active Chairman of the Board.

Jones' first practical truck refrigeration unit helped to completely change the food transport industry. It created new markets for many food crops, and influenced the eating habits of countless people. Frozen foods were now available to more individuals, and the refrigeration unit helped to save lives during World War II.

FROM RACING CARS TO REFRIGERATED TRUCKS

Frederick Jones became a top ranking engineer and inventor the hard way. He was an orphan for most of his boyhood. His mother had died when he was only an infant and his father when he was nine years old. After his father's death he left his birthplace, Cincinnati, Ohio, and went to live with a priest, Father Ryan, in Kentucky. Here he lived in a rectory where he did odd jobs for the priest and attended school through grade six. When Jones was 16, he decided to leave the priest who had raised him and began to look for a job.

When he left the rectory, the first big automobiles were beginning to appear. Jones was fascinated by these machines and hitched a ride in one at every chance. He developed a burning desire to work with them—to use his mind and his hands, and to touch the mechanical parts under the hood. He figured that the only way to do this was to get a job as an auto mechanic.

So, without experience or much education, he began his search. Jones returned to Cincinnati and finally convinced a garage owner that he was a skilled mechanic. The owner agreed to try him out on the following Monday morning. But Jones couldn't wait until then to get his hands on the cars and he showed up the next day, Saturday, at six, and waited for his new employer to open shop.

He had to prove himself at the thing that he wanted to do so badly. Although he didn't have much schooling, he had a keen inventive mind and an ability for understanding machinery. When he came to a problem in his work that stumped him, he went to the library and studied books on the subject. This became a habit of his and he practiced it throughout his life. Hard work and serious study paid off for the boy mechanic.

Three years later, Fred Jones became the foreman of the automobile shop. Now he wanted to work on racing cars. Auto racing was becoming a big sport at the time and the successful racer needed a car that would not fall apart at high speeds. Fred and his crew could take a bare chassis (car frame)—pull the steering wheel down to a sporty angle, change the gears, install a foot throttle and bucket seats, juggle some other parts around and wind up with a racer. He had built a couple of speedy racers by the time he was nineteen, but his boss thought he was too young to race and so others drove his cars instead.

One day Fred could not resist the temptation to be at the track to watch one of the cars he had built. He ducked out of the garage without his boss's permission and headed for the track. It was worth it to him since the racer he had worked on so hard and had kept in top condition won.

Fred's boss did not like the idea of him sneaking off and decided to lay him off for a while to teach him a lesson. This was hard for the young racing enthusiast to take. So he quit his job and headed for Chicago to see the sights of the big city.

On his way back to Cincinnati from Chicago, Fred Jones somehow boarded the wrong train. At daybreak he found himself in Effingham, Illinois. Being resourceful and curious, he decided to explore this unfamiliar town. And so he stayed in Effingham and managed to land a job fitting pipes together for a heating system being installed in a hotel near the train station. One of the hotel guests was a Mr. James Hill, who managed a 50,000 acre farm near Hallock, Minnesota. When the hotel-keeper heard that Hill was looking for a mechanic to keep his machinery in good condition he recommended that Hill talk with Fred Jones. Jones accepted the new challenge offered by Hill and on a snowy Christmas Day in 1912, he arrived in Hallock, Minnesota, his home for the next 18 years.

Steam engines, gasoline-driven tractors, hay loaders, cream separators, ditching and fencing machines, harvesters, and road graders; all this machinery and more were on the farm for Jones to work on. Mr. Hill also had several cars that had to be kept in good running order. There was plenty of work for the new mechanic, and plenty of opportunity for him to learn. He turned every new problem into a learning situation. After the sun went down he spent his time reading books on electricity, engines, and other subjects, adding more to his knowledge of mechanical engineering. Jones did more than just work and study. In Hallock he made many friends with whom he hunted and fished. He sang in the local town quartet and played the saxophone in the town band.

During World War I, Frederick Jones enlisted in the Army. He served in France as an electrician and earned the rank of sergeant. When the war ended, he returned to Hallock and became employed at a garage where cars, tractors, and farm machinery were repaired. He

Often Jones would race the cars he helped to build.

liked complicated jobs and would often make different parts out of scraps and pieces of old machinery. His new employer, Oscar Younggren, was a racing car "bug" and together they toured the dirt-track circuit. They whipped up a racer from a Dodge frame and engine, installed Hudson "super-six" valves, a Ford Model-T rear axle, and an oil pump from a Rumley tractor. Jones raced for a number of years and set several track records at county fairground events.

One day in 1925, Jones was scheduled for a five mile race. Three racers had already been killed in accidents that day at the track. Jones was nervous and once into his race he hit one turn at 100 miles per hour, sliding into a fence and clipping several posts before his car rolled to a stop. He was knocked unconscious and when he came to he found himself in an ambulance. His injuries were not severe, but that day finished Jones' career as an auto racer.

His imagination and ability led him on to other adventures. The first radios were beginning to come to Minnesota and he soon found himself surrounded with coils, tubes, and condensers. He bought books on electronics and the science of sound, and his self-education continued. When the publisher of the Hallock newspaper obtained a radio broadcasting license, Fred Jones built the first transmitter for the station. He built many table model radios for his friends in Hallock so they could listen to the local station.

Jones also worked at the Grand Theater in Hallock where he ran the movie projector. When "talking" movies became available, the theater owner realized that he would have to install sound equipment in order to continue to attract his customers. But he couldn't afford to buy the expensive equipment needed for sound films. So Jones offered to try to build some sound equipment himself. Using heavy steel disks from a plow, a leather machine belt, sprockets from an automobile piston, and some other odds and ends, Jones built a soundtrack unit that was as good as anything that could have been purchased. His device, which kept sound records in time with the moving film, cost less than $100 to make. The commercial outfits available at the time cost about $3,000.

But by 1930, most good motion pictures were made with the soundtrack on the film itself. Records which once provided the sound for movies were on their way out. Now the sound track was placed directly on the film and this meant that new equipment was necessary.

Again, Fred Jones decided to build his own device for combining sound with the film. Using information he gained from reading and his own creative ideas, he took a glass rod and ground it into the shape of a half cylinder. Then connecting the reshaped rod to a photoelectric cell he was able to produce a narrow beam of light. When the light hit the moving film the sound track was made audible. Within a short period of time, the Grand Theater in Hallock was in step with the modern "talking" movies.

News of Jones' work reached the ears of Joseph A. Numero in Minneapolis. Numero owned a company that manufactured motion picture equipment. He was having trouble constructing sound pickup devices and decided to invite Jones to Minneapolis to help him. Little did he realized that this invitation would result in the business of manufacturing refrigeration units for trucks and railway cars.

Fred Jones accepted Mr. Numero's job offer and he joined Cinema Supplies, Inc., in 1930. Sound equipment made by Numero's firm was soon used in movie houses throughout the northern Midwest and in 85 movie houses in Chicago. On June 27, 1939, Frederick Jones received his first patent for a Ticket Dispensing Machine for movie house tickets. An ex-racing car builder was now benefitting the movie business and contributing to the entertainment of thousands of Americans.

REFRIGERATION PIONEER

By the late 1930's, Jones was still working as an engineer for Numero's firm. Instead of movie house equipment,

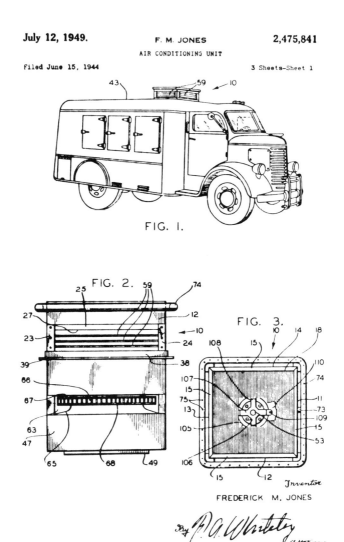

Figures two and three above illustrate Jones' patent for a removable cooling device. Figure one also indicates how the air conditioner is placed on top of the vehicle in order to take up less storage space.

however, he was busy designing portable air coolers for trucks that would carry perishable foods. The switch from the movie house supply business to cold boxes occurred soon after Jones invented the first truck air conditioner. Numero sold his interests in theatre equipment to RCA, and he and Jones devoted their full time to cold storage.

In 1949, the U. S. Thermo Control Company, founded jointly by Jones and Numero, had boomed to a $3,000,000 a year business. They manufactured automatic air coolers for trains, ships and airplanes so that foodstuffs could be kept fresh for long periods of time. And Jones was behind it all.

As an inventor he was never satisfied with the improvements he made in his cooling units. He developed ways that kept the air around the food at a constant temperature. He created other devices that produced special atmospheric conditions to keep strawberries and other fruits from drying out or becoming too ripe before reaching the supermarkets. Still other methods controlled the moisture in the air and air circulation. Jones' inventions made it possible for the first time to transport meat, fruit, vegetables, eggs, butter, and other produce that needed refrigeration over long distances during any season of the year.

In one of his applications to the United States Patent Office for a Removable Cooling Unit, Frederick Jones said the following:

> My invention relates to a removable cooling unit for compartments of trucks, railroad cars and the like employed in transport-

ing perishables and to a method of cooling such compartments and has for its object to provide a simple and compact self-contained cooling unit positioned at the top of said compartment and combined with air flow passages which produce a vortex of cold air flowing about the walls of the compartment and returning from the center of the compartment.

Perishables such as meats, vegetables, fruits, and the like are transported in what are known as refrigerator cars by rail and, to a greatly increased degree at the present time in trucks. This transportation, taking place as it does over long routes which in the summer time are at high temperatures throughout and even in winter time may be in part at high temperatures, requires artifical cooling in order to preserve said perishables in suitable condition for use as food.

In the case of refrigerator railroad cars, heavy cooling means such as large ice compartments or large and heavy refrigerating plants can be practically employed. This is not true of trucks where the necessary limitations of their use call for cooling means relatively low weight and so positioned as to take up as little as possible of the space within the transporting compartment.

It is a principle object of my invention therefore, to provide a cooling unit small in size and weight, and positioned, together with the air-conducting passages, so as to occupy substantially none of the storage space within the vehicle compartment.

It is a further object of my invention to provide a unit which shall be mounted in the front wall of the compartment partly outside and partly inside and having its top adjacent to the top wall of the compartment. . . .

With a few changes Jones portable cooling units were important to the United States military effort in World War II. He designed refrigerator units that were sent to army hospitals and battlefields in the South Pacific. The units were needed to keep blood serum for transfusions, medicines, and food at certain exact temperatures. Helicopters were used to transport his coolers to jungle outposts in the South Pacific islands. Others were used on airplanes that flew wounded soldiers home over the Pacific. Some of his units could even produce heat if it was needed.

During his lifetime, Frederick Jones was awarded more than 60 patents; 40 were for refrigeration equipment alone. Others were for portable X-ray machines, and sound equipment techniques for motion pictures. Jones also patented many of the special parts of his air cooling machines; the self-starting gasoline engine that turned his cooling units on and off, the reverse cycling mechanism for producing heat or cold, and devices for controlling air temperature and moisture.

At fifty years of age, Frederick Jones was one of the outstanding authorities in the field of refrigeration in the United States. In 1944, he was elected to membership in the American Society of Refrigeration Engineers. College graduated scientists and engineers welcomed the chance to work with and learn from him. During the 1950's, he was called to Washington to give advice on problems having to do with refrigeration. He was a consultant to both the Defense Department and the United States Bureau of Standards.

When Frederick McKinley Jones passed away in Minneapolis in 1961, his inventions were serving people throughout the world. He was a behind-the-scenes contributor to many of the luxuries of modern living.

JAN E. MATZELIGER

1852–1889

The Making of a Shoe

Take off one of your shoes. Look at it carefully. Your shoe has three basic parts: sole, heel and uppers. The uppers is the part that covers the top of your foot. Notice the shape of each part and how they are held together. It looks quite simple, just some sewing and a few nails. The history of this basic necessity is actually quite ancient, and at one time it was the result of many hours of hand labor.

For several thousand years, man has worn some form of shoe. Shoes are so familiar to us that we just accept them with very little thought. They are worn not only for their appearance but, more important, for the protection and comfort they give us.

One reason they are taken for granted is that we have so many of them. But this was not always so. Until about 100 years ago, there was no machinery for making shoes and all this work was done by hand. The tools used were the knife, the awl, and the hammer and they had changed little from the days of the early Egyptians. With these tools the shoemaker did well if he made one pair a day. Consequently, shoes were scarce, expensive, and only the rich owned more than one pair.

When Thomas Beard, a London shoemaker, arrived in Salem, Massachusetts, in 1629, he became one of the first American shoemakers. Beard did a brisk business and other European shoemakers followed him to North America. During the 1600's, skilled shoe craftsmen were scarce. Since the demand for shoes was great, America's pioneer shoemakers could charge high prices for their products. Then unskilled workers started to make shoes for themselves and others at a lower cost. This competition hurt the business of the professional shoemakers.

So, in 1648, the shoemakers in and around Boston, Massachusetts, formed a union to protect their trade. They called themselves the *Company of Shoemakers.* By the end of the 1600's, this union was turning out large quantities of shoes, even though they were still entirely handmade.

In the 1700's, Colonial America's shoemaking center shifted from Boston to Lynn, Massachusetts, a small town in the northeast. Shoes had been made there since 1630 and they were known for their high quality. Throughout the 1770's, shoemakers and apprentices flocked to the town to learn their trade. Many considered it an honor to be trained by the Lynn craftsmen.

Today, of course, shoes are made completely by machines. The change from handmade shoes to machine made ones was slow and gradual. Between 1850 and 1900, machinery step by step, replaced hand labor. The little shops and businesses scattered throughout New England tended to disappear, and were replaced by large power driven and machine equipped factories.

One of these machines—the shoe *lasting* machine— was invented by Jan E. Matzeliger. Matzeliger was a black man who lived and worked in Lynn as a shoe machine mechanic. His lasting machine replaced the only operation in shoe making that was still being done by hand, and it changed the industry more than any other machine. During his short lifetime he saw his invention increase shoe production tenfold while decreasing the man-hours of labor needed to make shoes. This resulted in lower cost to both the shoe manufacturer and the customer.

Before we take a closer look at Matzeliger's ingenious invention, let's find out what the terms "last" and "lasting" mean.

The *last* is a reproduction of the approximate shape of the human foot. Usually made from maple wood, the last was carved into a model of a customer's foot. A properly constructed shoe when made over this form will result in a shoe that supports and protects the foot without any pressure or binding. The last, therefore, is very important to the end result; the fitting, walking ease, and stylish appearance of a finished shoe depends upon it.

The word last comes from the Anglo-Saxon word "laest" which means a footprint, foot-track, or foot-trace. In colonial days, when a person was having a pair of shoes made he was not always around to try them on for size and fit, and so it was natural that some sort of form should be made on which to shape the shoe. It was equally natural to call this form or wooden shape by the word that meant a footprint or a foot-track. The French called it a "forme."

Today our shoes are still built on lasts. Lasts are made in many sizes by a machine. In the factory the last becomes the mold upon which the parts of the uppers are formed. They are the foundation of shoemaking— determining the size, shape, and fit of all footwear to be manufactured.

When Thomas Beard and other pioneer shoemakers came to America their shoemaking kit contained only the simplest of tools. Apparently Beard brought no lasts with him for there is mention that he "whittled his lasts from hard maple or hard wood." Going back much further into history, ancient shoe craftsmen made their shoes over lasts which were chiseled out of stone.

From the stone last age to present day methods is a long span of years. Yet the real progress began with the invention of the sewing machine in 1846 by Elias Howe. Shortly thereafter the Howe sewing machine was adapted to sew the various parts of a shoe together. In the next 17 years, many changes were made and many machines developed to make shoes; but no one designed a machine to last shoes—that is, to sew the uppers to the sole. Some inventors spent large amounts of money and time trying to invent a machine that would work successfully—but none succeeded. It seemed that the lastings of shoes would always remain a hand process.

Because of this fact, the hand lasters became the ruling craftsmen of the shoe workers. They were skillful, and they earned high wages. Most of them were proud of their position in the trade and even boasted about it.

In Lynn a laster was known to have voiced his opinion in these words:

> "No matter if the McKay sewing machine is a wonderful machine, no man can build a machine that will last shoes and take away the job of the laster unless he can make a machine that has fingers like a laster—and that's impossible."

The boast was heard by the young black mechanic who was operating a McKay machine in a Lynn shoe factory in 1880. Jan Matzeliger was to do what most felt —"couldn't be done." He designed a machine that would shape the upper leather over the last and attach this leather to the sole of the shoe with tacks.

Matzeliger's machine has been somewhat changed and improved, but its principle remains the same. Today, in Lynn and in other shoe manufacturing cities throughout the world, automatic tack lasters are in use.

FROM SOUTH AMERICA TO LYNN

On May 16, 1967, the city of Lynn honored its 19th century inventor. Sponsored by the local branch of the National Association for the Advancement of Colored People (NAACP), it was called Jan E. Matzeliger Day, and many citizens supported it. In the evening a banquet was held in honor of Matzeliger. Jackie Robinson, the first black man to play in professional baseball was the guest speaker.

Ninety years is a long time—more than the average lifetime. It is an especially long time to recall a person with a special day in his name. Matzeliger had come to Lynn some ninety years before the year in which he was honored. When he arrived in Lynn on a raw, chilly day back in the winter of 1877, he could barely speak the English language.

Jan Matzeliger was not a native American. He was born in Paramaribo, Surinam (Dutch Guiana), South

America, in 1852. His father was a Dutch engineer who had married a native black Surinamese woman. Her ancesters probably came from West Africa. Between 1650 and 1820, about 300,000 West Africans were brought to Dutch Guiana as slaves.

Matzeliger's father had been sent to Surinam by the Dutch government to direct the government machine work on the Dutch colony. At the age of ten, young Jan went to work in the machine shops supervised by his father. He learned rapidly and showed a definite talent for fixing and running machines.

In 1871, at the age of 19, the tall, slender mechanic left his homeland to travel and learn more about the world. He spent two years as a sailor on an East Indian merchantship. In 1873, when his ship docked in Philadelphia, young Matzeliger ended his seafaring life. Although he couldn't speak a word of English, he was a good mechanic and he managed to find several odd jobs—one working with a cobbler.

Little is known about Matzeliger's life in Philadelphia, except that he probably became a devout Christian during his years in this city. He must have heard about the rapid growth of the shoe industry in Massachusetts for more than half of the shoes being produced in the entire country at the time were coming from Lynn. Workers were constantly in demand and Europeans as well as the native born were quickly moving to shoe centers like Lynn to fill the job openings. Hoping for a better job, Matzeliger arrived in Lynn in 1877, alone and very poor.

Since he was a black foreigner, and hardly spoke any
English he had trouble getting a job. He went from factory to factory, only to be turned down each time. Shoe
factory owners saw little use for his background and
training. No one realized his ambition and inventive
mind would soon be all important to their industry.

Matzeliger was a determined young man, and not easily
discouraged. He quickly learned to speak and write the
English language. Eventually he landed a job as an ap-
prentice in a shoe factory operating a McKay-sole-sewing
machine. At night, after stitching shoes all day in the
factory, he attended evening school to continue his study
of English. Because of his natural mechanical ability,
Matzeliger became an important worker in the factory.
He took special interest in all the machines and hand
labor operations that went on around him. As he did his
daily sewing tasks he often thought about some of the
problems with the shoe machinery being used at the
time.

Other jobs followed. Although his days were busy and
long, he still found time on weekends to drive a coach
to and from a picnic park in West Lynn. He was gradually becoming settled in the community where he was
to spend the remainder of his short life. Wherever
Matzeliger worked he was modest, pleasant, and
friendly. At a time when most Lynn people were inclined
to look down on him because of his dark skin, he was
still able to make a few close friends. Matzeliger was a
religious man and he always wore a small medal in his
coat lapel which he brought from Philadelphia, inscribed

with the words—"Safe in Jesus." When he first tried to attend white churches in Lynn he was turned away because he was black. In 1884, he was welcomed by the Christian Endeavor Society, a young adult group, at the North Congregational Church. Although he was never an official member of this church, he regularly attended its Sunday services and taught Sunday school classes for the Society. Many of his church friends worked with Matzeliger in the factories of Lynn. Some of them felt he deserved more recognition than he was receiving.

Matzeliger became more and more fascinated with machinery. Being industrious he never stopped working and studying hard at his trade. He bought books on physics and mechanical science and his own drawing instruments and tools. His creative mind began to produce a variety of devices—an orange wrapping machine, a railroad car coupler, and some shoe machinery parts. Having little money, he was unable to patent and manufacture his first inventions. One of them, the railroad car coupler, came into general use only after his employer put up the money for its development and manufacture. Later, the employer claimed the patent for the device in his own name.

Matzeliger, however, had another idea by now; he was thinking about a machine that could last shoes.

IMITATING THE SHOE LASTERS HANDS

Labor conditions in Lynn at the time increased Matzeliger's interest in a possible lasting machine. The shoe lasters were organized into a union and were at the height of their power in 1877. They had frequent disputes with shoe manufacturers, and often went on strike to force their employers to meet their demands for more pay or better working conditions. When this happened all other departments of the factory came to a standstill, and other workers were left idle. The lasters felt they could do pretty much as they wished since there was no machine to take their place. This attitude irritated Matzeliger since he felt it was unfair that he and many others would be without work and wages for periods of time. He said he would put an end to the hand lasters rule by inventing a machine that would do their job perfectly. His fellow workers only jeered at him. Little did they realize that Matzeliger was serious about everything he attempted.

His problem was to design a successful machine that worked exactly like the hands of the skilled human laster. "I must carefully study the hands of a laster in action," he probably thought to himself, "and then recreate the movements of his hands with moving metal parts—gears, levers and cams." So he began to study the precise motions of the hand laster. He even got his job in the shoe factory changed so as to be near the lasting department.

It had not occurred to anyone else that this approach might bring success. Matzeliger started from scratch and worked alone. Consequently, he was not influenced from the ideas and mistakes of those who had tried before him.

There was still much opposition to machinery replacing people in the factories, so Matzeliger decided that he would do his work secretly. He rented a room over the old West Lynn Mission. Here he could hide while he made sketches and experimented with his models. During the day he would study the hand lasters at work. His keen eyes followed their exact finger movements and he noted the way one hand operated in time with the other. Lasting was a job for strong hands. It required constant pulling in a circular motion as the leather on the upper part of the shoe was tacked on to the insole. Matzeliger quietly watched this go on hour after hour each day as he worked. When his day at the factory was over he would return to his rented room and work far into the night. The laster's union was very powerful and had they known what he was doing, they probably would have had him fired.

He started by making rough drawings of machine parts and how they fitted together. From his drawings he went to pieces of cardboard pivoting on pins. Each hand movement had to be imitated. Soon a crude model began to take shape. Made of parts cut from old cigar boxes, pieces of wood, bits of wire, and nails, it performed the movements he thought were necessary. This first model took six months to build.

Despite his secrecy, word about what he was doing in the room over the Mission leaked out. People, when they saw his model, laughed at the "funny looking thing made from scraps of cardboard, wood, wire and nails." Some people warned him how others had tried and failed, and very few encouraged him. Matzeliger needed money to continue his work but could find no one to support him. One man who had been trying to invent a lasting machine for years offered Matzeliger $50 for his first rough model. He was ready to sell it but changed his mind at the last minute. This bit of interest by another inventor assured Matzeliger that he was on the right track. He was determined to perfect his first attempt.

The second model had to be made of metal parts. Matzeliger began to collect bits of scrap metal and the discarded parts of old broken down machines. But now that he was going to work his idea into metal, he needed a machine shop in which to continue his experimentation. He managed to acquire a small space in the factory where he was employed. Each night he worked away at his model, forging, filing, machining, and fitting. It was extremely hard work but he continued alone. After four years Matzeliger was a tired man. He was poor too, since he had been spending all of his earnings on his machine. He often denied himself good meals, and spent his daily wages on his machine rather than food. Often he ate nothing but corn meal mush.

Matzeliger's patient and exhausting years of work resulted in an improved, but still crude model. The lack of money was a real problem now that he had completed it. Cash was needed to get a patent and to arrange for the completion of the machine so that it could be tried out in a factory. Some offers came in to buy the rights to parts of the machine—$1,500 for the part that turned the leather around the toe of the shoe. With this offer, Matzeliger was even more convinced that he had the beginnings of a great invention. He wanted investors that would back the whole machine. Finally he found two

J. E. MATZELIGER
LASTING MACHINE

No. 274,207.   PATENTED MAR. 20, 1883

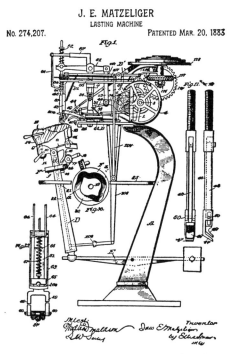

Matzeliger's model and patent of his lasting machine was a breakthrough for mass producing shoes.

wealthy Lynn citizens willing to put up the money. Matzeliger set out to build an improved third model. For their financing the investors gained ownership of two-thirds of the invention.

When his third model was finished, he applied for a patent. Patents were usually given on the basis of detailed drawings sent to the United States Patent Office in Washington, D.C. After studying Matzeliger's drawings, Patent Office officials could hardly believe that a machine could do what Matzeliger claimed his could do. A representative of the Patent Office came to Lynn to examine Matzliger's model. Finally, in March of 1883, Jan E. Matzeliger was awarded Patent No. 274,207 for his "Lasting Machine." However, he was still not completely satisfied with his work. After testing his machine under factory conditions he found that many improvements were still necessary. And so he worked for two more years on experiments and test runs. By the spring of 1885 he was ready to factory test a much simplified and improved machine. On May 29, his machine lasted 75 pairs of women's shoes perfectly. It passed the factory test.

Suddenly Matzeliger had many friends. Organizations with money to invest and companies already in the shoe machinery business wanted to exploit his invention and gain quick and huge profits. The outcome was the formation of the Consolidated Lasting Machine Company. This company took over Matzeliger's patents for which he received a large block of stock in the company. The Company immediately began rapid production of the new machine. Matzeliger's hand-method laster was on its way to revolutionizing shoe manufacturing. The 225 workers building the Matzeliger machine lasters at the Consolidated plant could hardly keep up with orders for the machine.

An expert hand laster working ten hours a day could produce about fifty pairs of shoes. Matzeliger's laster could turn out from 150 to 700 pairs each day depending on the quality of work. By 1889 the demand for the shoe lasting machine was overwhelming. The Consolidated

Company had to set up a school in Lynn where hand lasters and others could learn how to operate the new machine.

While the merits of Matzeliger's invention were recognized by shoe manufacturers as a boon to their business, to the hand lasters, it was a threat. It broke the power of their union because unskilled workers at lower wages could be hired to operate the machine.

Naturally, the lasters opposed the machine. Its inventor was a black man and the lasters scornfully called it "The Nigger-Head Machine." They ridiculed it whenever possible.

One tale, often heard around Lynn in the early 1900's was started by an old laster. The "Nigger Machine," he said, had human fingers that worked with human intelligence and it actually talked; the sounds coming from the machine when in operation seemed to echo the words: "I've got your job. I've got your job."

Below is part of an article that appeared in the *Lynn Item* on October 3, 1899. It helps to tell the rest of the Matzeliger story.

"Nearly every factory in Lynn is introducing the hand-method lasting or 'niggerheads,' and dropping hand lasting or the tack driving machines which were merely aids to the hand laster. . . .

There are many firms which cling to some of the other lasting machines, but most of the factories are discarding them for the hand method machine, and in fact will be forced to do so within a short time, as this is the only lasting machine manufactured today to any extent. In the consolidation of the shoe lasting machinery companies all the lasting machinery in America were brought under the control of the one firm, and all the later inventions have been found inferior to the first lasting machine which was made, the 'niggerhead,' invented by a South American Negro, Matzeliger, employed in a Lynn shoe factory."

MATZELIGER'S LEGACY

Jan Matzeliger did not live to see the results of his hard work and creativity. Sadly too, he never enjoyed the fame and fortune that he deserved. He had driven himself too hard. His body was weak from the strain of overworking, often going without enough sleep and food. Sundays had been his only day of relaxation, when he attended church and taught Sunday school.

On a chilly, wet day in 1886, Matzeliger caught cold. The cold lingered on and developed into something more serious. He became bedridden. His condition became worse and he moved from his room over the Mission to a home where friends could care for him. Finally his illness was diagnosed as tuberculosis. A doctor ordered Matzeliger to the Lynn Hospital where he was to spend his last days. On August 24, 1889 when only 37 years old, Jan E. Matzeliger died.

Four months before his death, Matzeliger made out his will. In it he remembered everyone who had been close to him. To 15 of his friends, his hospital doctor, and Lynn Hospital, he left blocks of Consolidated stock. To others he left his gold watch and chain, the watercolors done during his years of illness, his Bibles, and the drawing instruments that he used to sketch the designs of his invention.

The greatest benefactor in Matzeliger's will was the North Church of Lynn. When other church groups had rejected him upon his arrival in Lynn as a non-English speaking immigrant, it was the North Church that befriended him. To this church he left all of his stock in the Union Lasting Machine Company and one-third of his stock in the Consolidated Company.

In 1904, the North Congregational Church sold part of the stock that Matzeliger had willed to it for $10,000. This money made it possible for the church to pay off all of its mortgages. Years later, the North Church merged with another Lynn church to become the First Church of Christ.

In the First Church of Christ, at the morning services on Sunday, September 8, 1968, remembrance was given to Jan Matzeliger. The church bulletin that the parishoners received that morning contained the following:

> We are taking a few minutes this morning to honor the life of Jan Ernst Matzeliger. Jan Matzeliger's invention of the shoe lasting machine was perhaps the most important invention for New England. His invention was the greatest forward step in the shoe industry. Yet, because of the color of his skin, he was not mentioned in the major history books of the United States. . . .
>
> It was the sales of some more of his stocks which helped to make it possible to have this present church. We are not honoring Matzeliger because he gave the church money, but because he is a hero with whom the American people can identify.

LEWIS H. LATIMER

1848–1928

A Pioneer in Electric Lighting

... I was one of the pioneers of the electric lighting industry from its creation until it had become worldwide in its influence... This statement was made by a black man, Lewis H. Latimer. Not only was he an inventor who worked with Thomas Edison, inventor of the first practical electric light bulb, but he also drew the plans for Alexander Graham Bell's first telephone patent.

Lewis H. Latimer was the only black member of the Edison Pioneers, a group of distinguished scientists and inventors who worked for Thomas Edison. Edison used a teamwork approach in solving scientific and technological problems. His laboratories in Menlo Park and West Orange, New Jersey, became models for the huge industrial research centers that have become so important in our twentieth century American life. Today the team approach to scientific discovery and technology is widely used.

Edison's most important single invention was his incandescent light bulb. As an inventor of certain light bulb parts and a valuable member of Edison's team, Lewis Latimer helped to make the Edison lighting system possible.

When Latimer died in December, 1928, the Edison Pioneers released a statement to the press about his life and his contributions to the field of electric lighting. Part of the press release read as follows:

"... Mr. Latimer successfully produced a method of making carbon filaments for the Maxim electric incandescent lamp, which he patented. His keen perception of the possibility of the electric light and kindred industries resulted in his being the author of several other inventions. . . . In 1884, he became associated with the engineering department of the Edison Electric Light Company. . . . He was of the colored race, the only one in our organization, and was one of those to respond to the initial call that led to the formation of the Edison Pioneers, January 24, 1918. Broadmindedness, versatility in the accomplishment of things intellectual and cultural, a linguist, a devoted husband and father, all were characteristic of him, and his genial presence will be missed from our gatherings. . . ."

SON OF FUGITIVE SLAVES

During the 1800's, thousands upon thousands of black people escaped from legal slavery in the South by fleeing to northern states. George Latimer was one such slave who escaped from Virginia to gain freedom and to find a new life in Boston, Massachusetts. Here he met and married another fugitive slave from Virginia. They had four children, three boys and one girl. Lewis H. Latimer, born in September 1848, was the youngest of the family.

From his boyhood background it is unlikely that anyone would have predicted fame for the youngest son of two fugitive slaves. While Lewis attended elementary school in Boston he also worked a few hours each day in his father's barbershop. Later, when his father became a paperhanger, young Lewis worked with him at night and became quite an expert at paperhanging. At the age of ten, he left school and began working a full day helping his father.

Then for some unknown reason, George Latimer left home, deserting his wife and four children. This left Lewis' mother unable to support her children. Mrs.

Latimer sent her daughter to live with a friend and her two oldest sons to a farm school for boys in the western part of Massachusetts. Lewis remained in his mother's home until she got a chance to go to sea as a ship's stewardess. Then he, too, was sent to the same school as his brothers. They were no longer there, although one of them was working nearby at a hotel.

Lewis remained at the farm school for several years until one day his brother William returned for a visit and was surprised to find him at the school. William suggested that they run away and return to their native Boston. This appealed to Lewis since he longed to be free and wanted a job where he could use his mind instead of his muscles.

Boston was 84 miles away. Lewis and his brother planned their escape carefully, fearing that along the way they might be chased and caught by the school authorities. Running, walking, stealing rides on the railway, and begging for food along the way, Lewis and his brother arrived in Boston several days after fleeing the farm school. Perhaps now he knew how his mother and father had felt when they escaped from slavery in Virginia.

BECOMING A DRAFTSMAN

Back in Boston, and only 13 years old, Lewis moved from one odd job to another. He worked first as an office boy in a law office and later waited tables in the home of a wealthy Roxbury family.

In 1863, shortly after the Civil War began, Lewis Latimer was 15 years old. He was tired of Boston and working at odd jobs. Both of his brothers had joined the Navy, so Lewis, pretending to be older than he was, enlisted also. He served as a cabinboy on the *S.S. Massasoit* At the end of the war in 1865, Latimer returned to Boston and was honorably discharged.

After many weeks of trying to find work he secured a position as an office boy with the firm of Crosby and Gould, Patent Solicitors. His pay was three dollars a week. He worked in a large room filled with drafting tables. Men, leaning over the tables for hours, made detailed drawings of inventions. The work of the patent draftsman fascinated Lewis Latimer. As he watched them making drawings of inventions for the United States Patent Office, he noted what books they used. Later at a second hand book store, he purchased some that gave drawing instructions. Then with more of his savings, he was able to buy a set of drawing instruments. Each day as he moved around the office he looked over the draftsmen's shoulders to see how they used their tools.

In the evening he practiced and practiced and practiced—making drawings like those of the professional draftsmen he saw during the day. He was determined to be as good as they were.

Arriving at work one morning, young Latimer asked one of the draftsmen if he could do some drawing for him. At first the draftsman laughed but then decided to see what the office boy could do at the drawing board. He handed Lewis a piece of drawing paper and left him alone with an assignment. When the draftsman returned he was surprised to see how well he could draw. So from time to time he let Lewis do some of the work.

One day Lewis' boss saw him at the drawing board and was so pleased with his work that he was promoted from office boy to junior draftsman. Lewis began drawing eight hours a day. Often he made working models of inventions to go along with a drawing required by the Patent Office. Lewis stayed with Crosby and Gould for eleven years and when he left he was making $80 a week.

In 1876, Alexander Graham Bell applied for a United States Patent on his telephone. Bell was teaching sign language to deaf people in Boston and his school was near the offices of Crosby and Gould. Bell came to their office to have his patent drawings made, and Latimer was assigned to draw his telephone system.

Latimer later recalled his first meeting with the famous Bell—"He (Bell) was teaching day and night classes and I was obliged to stay at the office until after 9 PM . . . to get my instructions from him, as to how I was to make the drawings for the application for a patent upon the telephone."

At 30 years of age Lewis Latimer had become a skilled and respected draftsman of patents in line and color. He knew a great deal about the science of invention for he had an active and creative mind; and yet he wasn't satisfied with his accomplishments. He wanted to do more and he felt that many of the inventions that he had drawn could be improved upon. Latimer's dream was to become an inventor himself.

LATIMER ENTERS
THE WORLD OF ELECTRIC LIGHTING

In 1879, Lewis Latimer left Boston and went to Bridge-port, Connecticut, to live with his married sister. His first job was in a machine shop making mechanical drawings. When Hiram Maxim, inventor of the machine gun, entered the shop one day, he was surprised to see a drafts-man who was black. He was further amazed to see the fine drawings that Latimer was making. At the time Maxim was the Chief Engineer of the United States Electrical Lighting Company. He had been looking for a draftsman to do patent drawings and he soon realized Latimer was his man. While working for Maxim as a mechanical draftsman and secretary, Latimer quickly learned everything he could about electric light con-struction and operation. In 1879, Thomas Edison in-vented an electric light and Latimer began to experiment with some ways to improve Edison's lamp.

In the early spring of 1880, Maxim moved his com-pany to New York City and Latimer moved on with him. When he wasn't drawing, he was put in charge of produc-ing the carbon filaments for electric lamps. The filament is the material in a light bulb that glows when an electric current passes through it.

For about 26 years all light bulbs (incandescent lamps) had carbon filaments. They were made by burning cellu-lose found in paper, bamboo or cotton thread. Cellulose is composed largely of carbon combined with other ele-ments, usually hydrogen and oxygen. When cellulose is

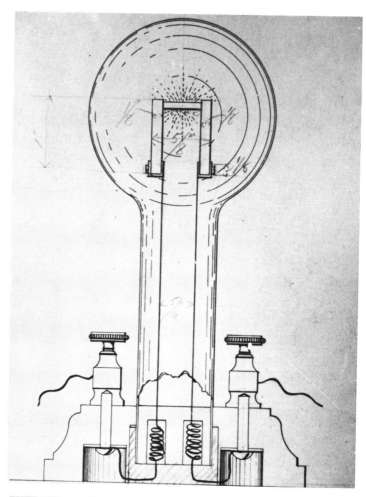

The first drawing made by me for Hiram Stevens Maxim was made from this drawing in Bridgeport Conn in 1880

S. H. Latimer.

heated slowly in a closed furnace without air, it breaks down. The hydrogen, oxygen and some of the carbon is driven off. A carbon skeleton remains. This carbon skeleton, which is very hard and dense like coal, becomes the filament material for the electric lamp.

In an incandescent lamp, the electric current heats to an almost white heat. This almost white heat gives off the light we see. The hotter the filament is heated, the more light it radiates; also the hotter the filament is heated the sooner it wears out. Edison felt that a good filament should last 600 hours. So Latimer worked very hard to improve the quality of the filament material. Gradually, the operating temperatures were raised with no loss to the life of the filament.

While working for Hiram Maxim, Latimer successfully produced a method of making an improved and cheaper carbon filament for Maxim's electric lamp. This improved carbon filament made it possible to operate lights safely at a high temperature. It also enabled more people to install them and to have electric lighting. Then in January, 1882, Latimer received his own patent on his electric light filament.

It wasn't long before this young black inventor was made chief electrical engineer for Maxim's company. He assisted in installing for operation some of the first "Maxim" incandescent electric light plants in New York City, Philadelphia, and Canada. At the same time, he supervised the production of the carbon filaments made by his own process. His lamps lit the railroad stations in Montreal and New York City.

Later, Latimer was sent to London, England, to establish an incandescent lamp factory for Maxim's company. Here he instructed workmen in every aspect of light bulb making, including the art of blowing glass.

Returning to the United States a year later, Lewis worked for two other companies. Shortly afterwards he designed and manufactured a lamp which bears his name and can be found in a famous collection of incandescent lamps at the Henry Ford Museum in Dearborn, Michigan. The Latimer Lamp is one of 800 lamps in the collection. Nearly all of them are very early examples of the beginning development in our electric lighting systems.

In 1884, Lewis received an important call from Edison's company. He was offered a job as a draftsman in the Engineering Department at the Edison offices in New York City. This was the beginning of Latimer's long association with Thomas Edison. He became a draftsman in the legal department and remained there for 30 years.

In Latimer's time, as it still is today, inventors must protect their patented inventions from being stolen and manufactured by others for profit. Some men claimed that they had developed lamps similar to Edison's and had done so earlier. They organized companies and produced lamps according to the principles in Edison's patents. The legal department of Edison's company was set up to protect his many electrical inventions. Sometimes a court case resulted over an argument on who had rights to a certain invention. Latimer often made drawings for court exhibits. He traveled around the country inspecting patents on electric lamps and gathered information on people who tried to steal patents that belonged to the Edison company. The court cases were long, drawn out legal battles and many times Latimer was the star witness. Edison usually won his cases and Latimer's knowledge of electrical patents and the Edison system were responsible for many of the victories.

A PUBLISHED ACCOUNT

Latimer was a great admirer of Thomas Edison and his work. And he wanted everyone to know about electric lighting. So, in 1890, Latimer wrote the first book on electric lighting. His book entitled, *Incandescent Electric Lighting*, was a practical description of the Edison system.

In his book, Latimer described how light is produced by heating a filament to incandescence. After discussing the various parts of the electric light, he wrote the following:

". . . If the electric current can be forced through a substance that is a poor conductor, it will create a degree of heat in that substance, which will be greater or less according to the quality of electricity forced through it.

Upon this principle of the heating effect of the electrical current, is based the operation of the incandescent lamp just described. While copper and platinum wires readily conduct the current, the carbon filament offers a great deal of resistance to its passage, and for this reason becomes very hot, in fact is raised to white heat or incandescence, which gives its name to the lamp. You doubtless wonder why this thread of charcoal is not immediately consumed when in this state, but this is really accounted for when you remember, that without oxygen of the air. there can be no combustion, and that every possible trace of air has been removed from the bulb and is so thoroughly sealed up as to prevent admission of the air about it; and yet the lamp does not last forever, for the reason that the action of the current upon the carbon has a tendency to divide up its particles and transfer them from one point to another so that, sooner or later, the filament gives way at some point. Yet most of these lamps are guaranteed to last a thousand hours, and this at from four to six hours a day gives the lamp a life of several months."

LATIMER—A BRIGHT LIGHT

Lewis Latimer did more than just help to bring electric light to the streets of New York, office buildings, and homes, subway stations, and railroad cars. Through his many activities and interests he brought "light" to the lives of those around him. He worked hard for civil rights organizations and taught immigrants the English language in a New York City community center.

Latimer expressed himself in other ways, too. When he had time he painted and wrote music and poetry. One of his poems—Keep In Touch With the World—gives a feeling for the type of person that Lewis Latimer actually was.

KEEP IN TOUCH WITH THE WORLD

Keep in touch with the world;
The days that are ours,
Are fleeting and soon
The night will be here.
If we've loved we have lived,
Midst its weeds and its flowers,
Midst its smiles and its laughter
As well as its tear.

Chorus.
Keep in touch with the world;
With its joys and its sorrows.
Keep in touch with the world;
With its pleasure and pain;
With its crime and its care,
For who knows but to-morrow
We may leave it to never
Return here again.

Those only who suffer,
Can feel for each other.
Experience is teaching
As naught else can teach.
Each woman's our sister,
Each man is our brother.
To tell of our love,
Is the purpose of speech.

Keep in touch with the world;
From the babe with its mother
To the tottering man
Deep wrinkled and gray.
To love while we live
And give aid to each other
Is the sunshine of life
That turns night into day.

ELIJAH McCOY

1843–1929

It's The Real McCoy

Have you ever wondered where the phrase "the real McCoy" came from? How it came to be part of our language? Its origin can be traced back to a young black American who was a mechanic in the early 1870's. His name was Elijah McCoy.

As a young man McCoy became fascinated with steam engines and he began experimenting with them. During this period of history most machines had to be stopped every time they needed oiling. Furthermore, the lubrication was done by hand oilers. Stopping and starting engines to oil them wasted a lot of time and it was also very expensive. McCoy realized that somehow a way had to be found to provide a continuous flow of oil on the moving parts of a machine while it was still operating.

So McCoy developed a small cup with a stopcock that could supply oil, drop by drop, to the moving parts of machines. This eliminated costly and time consuming stoppages for lubrication. McCoy's cup was extensively used on stationary engines and locomotives of the great railways in the West, on engines of steamships on the Great Lakes, on transatlantic liners, and on machinery in factories. No piece of heavy machinery was considered to be complete unless it was equipped with the McCoy lubricator.

Eventually railroad and factory inspectors, when checking out a new piece of machinery, began to ask, "Is it the real McCoy?" The phrase caught on and spread and was understood to mean "the real thing." It wasn't long before people began to apply the expression to many things besides machinery.

In his letter of application to the U.S. Patent Office for a patent on one of his first lubricators, McCoy wrote the following in describing how his lubricator worked.

To all whom it may concern:
Be it known that I, Elijah McCoy, of Ypsilanti, in the county of Washtenaw and in the State of Michigan, have invented certain

A new method of lubricating machines was developed by Elijah McCoy. The patent for this device is explained on the following page in McCoy's own words. Match the letters in the explanation with those in the drawing.

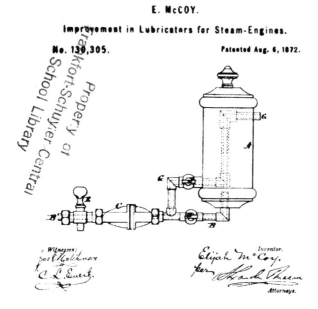

E. McCOY.

Improvement in Lubricators for Steam-Engines.

No. 130,305.   Patented Aug. 6, 1872.

new and useful Improvements in a Lubricator for Cylinders; and do hereby declare that the following is a full, clear, and exact description thereof, reference being had to the accompanying drawing and to the letters of reference marked thereon, making a part of the specification. . . .

A represents the vessel in which oil is contained, and from the bottom of which a pipe, B, leads to the steam-chest. This pipe is, at a suitable point, provided with a globe or reservoir, C. Between the vessel A and the globe or reservoir C is a stopcock, D, in the pipe B, and in the same pipe, between the globe and the steam-chest, is another stop-cock, E. A steampipe, G, passes from the dome or boiler down through the vessel and connects with the oil-pipe B at the glove or reservoir C, or at any point between the same and the valve D. In the steam-pipe G, after it leaves the vessel A, is a stop-cock, J. One of these oilers is to be placed on each side of the smoke-arch directly opposite the cylinder, and the various stop-cocks should be so connected with levers or rods that they can be operated simultaneously by a single rod in the engineer's cab. When the engine is working the stop-cocks E and J are closed and the stop-cock D opened, allowing the oil to pass into the globe or reservoir C. The steam being in the pipe G prevents the oil from congealing in cold weather in the vessel A. When the cylinder is to be oiled the stop-cocks E and J are opened and D closed. Steam passing from the boiler or dome through the pipe G forces the oil out of the globe or reservoir C into the cylinder. . . .

Elijah McCoy lived most of his life in Detroit, Michigan. Almost anyone who lived there between 1882 and 1929 had heard something about McCoy, but there were few people who knew him well. Occasionally, in answer to a question about McCoy one would say, "Oh, he's the one that invented some kind of lubricator, isn't he?" Beyond this most people knew very little or nothing about him.

FROM CANADA TO DETROIT

McCoy was born in May, 1843, in Colchester, Ontario, Canada. Both of his parents, who had been slaves in Kentucky, escaped to Canada in the Fall of 1837 via the Underground Railroad. The Railroad as we said before, was the network of homes and farms where antislavery people in America hid escaping southern slaves and helped them on their way to freedom in the North and in Canada.

After settling in Canada, McCoy's father joined the Canadian Army. He served the British government and upon his honorable discharge was given 160 acres of farmland in Colchester. Elijah attended school and worked on his father's farm until he was 15 years old.

After his fifteenth birthday his father sent him to Edinburgh, Scotland, to study mechanical engineering. After five years in Scotland, Elijah returned to Canada as a master mechanic and engineer. He worked there for a year and then left for the United States to find a job.

The best offer that he could get was that of a railroad fireman. A bit discouraged, he still took the job and began work on the Michigan Central Railroad. At this time wood was used as fuel and men stood on the running board to pour oil from cups onto the steam chest of the engine. McCoy felt that there must be a better way to lubricate machines. So his mechanical mind started to work.

Around 1870, McCoy was living in Ypsilanti, Michigan, where he began experimenting in his machine shop with lubricators for steam engines. After two years of labor, on June 23, 1872, he received his first patent for a locomotive lubricator. But he was not satisfied with his first try, as he wanted to perfect his ideas. In the next few years McCoy obtained six patents for different types of lubricators, and during his lifetime he received a total of 57.

At first, locomotive engineers objected to using McCoy's new invention on their engines simply because a black man had invented them. Many of the men ridiculed McCoy and called his lubricator a "nigger oilcup."

Despite the objections however, the "nigger oilcup," was installed on locomotives under the direct supervision of McCoy himself. And it was not unusual for the engineers to be instructed by him on how to use it. From 1872 to 1915, most of the railroad locomotives in the United States and in foreign countries as well were equipped with McCoy's lubricators.

THE McCOY GRAPHITE LUBRICATOR

From 1882 to 1926, 45 patents were awarded to Elijah McCoy. All but eight of them pertained to lubricating devices.

McCoy considered his Graphite Lubricator, patented in April, 1915, to be his best invention. About 1920, he organized the Elijah McCoy Manufacturing Company in Detroit to manufacture and sell this lubricator. It was designed to overcome the difficulties in oiling an engine called a superheater which operated by using large amounts of steam.

Before McCoy developed his Graphite Lubricator, the problems of lubricating the superheater engine were made clear by a Mr. Kelly in an article in the *Engineer's Journal*. Mr. Kelly wrote:

There is Need of a Remedy

"There is no denying the fact that our present experience in lubricating the cylinders of engines using superheated steam is anything but satisfactory. Locomotive Superintendents and Master Mechanics are trying to make each other and everyone else believe that they have solved the problem, but perfect lubrication cannot be had unless there is provision made to supply the oil to cylinder with some degree of regularity. . . . If the oil feed was made regular so the steam would distribute it over the bearing surface of cylinder when engine is working, these bearing surfaces would be better protected than is now otherwise possible.

"Our trouble from trying to lubricate cylinders of superheated engines are not so much due to lack of an oil to withstand the heat of cylinders as to a lack of some way to supply the oil we have with some regularity while the engine is working.

In 1914 McCoy filed a letter of application for a patent on a lubricator that used a solid substance called graphite as the lubricant. Graphite is a form of the element carbon and is the basic substance found in the lead of an ordinary pencil. If you were to rub some powdered graphite between your fingers, you would find it is soft, smooth, and greasy. Because of these properties, graphite makes an ideal lubricant. Perhaps you have lubricated bicycle parts or locks with this powdered material. Sometimes it is mixed with oil or water as it was in McCoy's lubricator.

Here is what McCoy said in part of his letter of application for a patent:

To all whom it may concern:

Be it known that I, Elijah McCoy, a citizen of the United States of America, residing in Detroit, in the county of Wayne and State of Michigan, have invented certain new and useful Improvements in Locomotive-Lubricators, of which the following is a specification, reference being had therein to the accompanying drawings.

McCoy invented a graphite lubricator for use on railroad loco-motives with superheater engines. It provided a continuous flow of oil without clogging the engine.

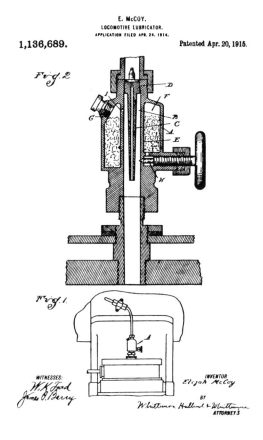

E. McCOY.
LOCOMOTIVE LUBRICATOR.
APPLICATION FILED APR. 24, 1914.

1,136,689.

Patented Apr. 20, 1915.

Fig. 2

Fig. 1

WITNESSES:
W. K. Ford
James O. Barry

INVENTOR
Elijah McCoy
BY
Whittemore Hulbert & Whittemore
ATTORNEYS

The invention relates to locomotive lubricators and it is the particular object of the invention to provide means for introduction of graphite or other suspended solid lubricant without danger of clogging.

In the drawings; Figure 1 is an elevation of my improved lubricator, showing it as applied to a locomotive; and fig. 2 is a longitudinal section thereof.

In the present state of the art, locomotive lubricators are usually provided with a restricted passage or choke-plug, which is arranged adjacent to the steam chest at the lower end of the oil conduit. This choke-plug is usually a separate fitting which has a screw threaded engagement with the nipple entering the steam chest and a union coupling with the oil conduit. This is adapted for the feeding of a free-flowing oil, but a heavy lubricant and particularly one containing a suspended solid matter, such as graphite, is liable to obstruct the choke-plug so as to render the device inoperative.

With my improved construction, means is provided for feeding the heavy lubricant without danger of obstructing this choke-plug, this consisting essentially of a lubricant cup associated with a choke-plug, but so as not to clog the restricted passage.

From reading the reports below you can get some idea how effective McCoy's Graphite lubricator was and how it met the need that Mr. Kelly described.

What Users Think of the McCoy Graphite Lubricator

Answering an inquiry regarding the McCoy Graphite Lubricator, the Superintendent of Motive Power of one of the large Central Railroads writes:

"We have found the McCoy Graphite Lubricator to be of considerable assistance in lubrication of locomotives equipped with superheaters. . . . There is a decided advantage in better lubrication and reduction in wear in valves and piston rings, and as a well lubricated engine is more economical in the use of fuel, there is unquestionably a saving in fuel."

The Best Thing in the World

Under date of April 12, 1918, the Master Mechanic of a well known Canadian Road on being asked how he liked the McCoy Graphite Lubricator, said, "It is the best thing in the world, as it saves us a world of trouble," and later in writing to the McCoy Company under date of July 19, 1918, "I am very much interested in your graphite lubricator as it is giving good service."

By 1923, Elijah McCoy was well known throughout the mechanical-industrial world. His many inventions carried patents in many foreign countries—Great Britain, France, Germany, Austria, and Russia. He was often called upon as a consultant to give advice to large industrial concerns.

Elijah was also well known among the youth of Detroit. He counseled teenage boys and had no patience with a young dude who put everything upon his back and nothing in his head. He felt that what he had accomplished, thousands of others could also, if only they would apply themselves. At eighty years of age McCoy stood perfectly erect and was remarkably active. He was proud of his inventions and the fact that he could still touch his toes without bending his knees.

Sometime after 1926, McCoy's health began to fail. He was alone during his last days, his wife having died a few years earlier. In 1928 he was admitted to Eloise Infirmary in Eloise, Michigan, where he died in 1929.

McCoy's accomplishments during extremely difficult times for black Americans are examples of persistence. When no positions were open to him despite the fact that he was a trained engineer, he took the nearest thing to an engineer that he could get, that of a fireman, and made the best of his opportunity. The result was a teacher of engineers and a master of master mechanics. Daily papers and mechanical and engineering journals spoke highly of his work. His patents were used internationally and his inventions contributed to the growth of our nation. Elijah McCoy was as real as his work.

NORBERT RILLIEUX

1806–1894

"A Sweeter Life"

It has been estimated that each person in the United States uses about 100 pounds of sugar a year. Yet, like many of the things that you use each day, you probably take sugar for granted. It is one of our most important foods, for it provides quick energy and heat for the body. However, during most of the 1800's, sugar was a luxury. Few people could afford it and for those who could, it was hard to get. The manufacturing process that changed the juice from the sugar cane plant into sugar was slow and expensive.

During the 1800's and early 1900's many books and articles were written about the history of sugar manufacturing and refining. If you were to look at some of these, the name Rillieux would often appear. In 1846, Norbert Rillieux received a United States patent for an invention first used in a sugar factory near New Orleans, Louisiana. Rillieux had found a new way of turning sugar juice into a fine grade of white sugar crystals. The device that he developed was known as the *multiple-effect vacuum evaporator*. Basically, this process of his is still used throughout the sugar industry today.

Rillieux's evaporator greatly reduced the production cost and provided a superior grade of sugar. Sugar manufacturers proclaimed Rillieux's invention as a revolution in the processing of raw sugar. His method was quickly adopted by Cuban and Mexican sugar refineries and he soon became the most famous engineer in the state of Louisiana.

Most historians who wrote about the development of the sugar industry have failed to mention that Rillieux was a black American, although they were generous in their praise of his contribution. J. G. McIntosh, in his book *Technology of Sugar* (1903), gave five pages to the development, principle, and advantages of Rillieux's evaporator. He said, "This is a system which constitutes the basis of all the saving in fuel hitherto effected in sugar factories . . . Rillieux may, therefore, with all justice, be regarded as one of the greatest benefactors of the sugar industry."

Another writer and authority, Charles A. Browne, an outstanding sugar chemist with the United States Department of Agriculture, had this to say: "I have always held that Rillieux's invention is the greatest in the history of American chemical engineering, and I know of no other invention that has brought as great a saving to all branches of chemical engineering." Rillieux's invention was universally used throughout the sugar industry and also in the manufacturing of condensed milk, soap, gelatin, and glue. The underlying principle has not changed much since he first designed his system in the 1840's.

THE MANUFACTURING OF SUGAR

It should be made clear before going any further, that sugar is not really manufactured in a sugar factory. Actually, it is made by green plants. A plant's green leaves using the energy of sunlight makes sugar from water taken from the soil and carbon dioxide from the air. This process is called photosynthesis, which means—manufactured—or put together by light. Table sugar, or sucrose, as it is called by scientists, is the most famous of many natural plant substances called sugars. And the substance you use on your food has the same chemical makeup as the one naturally made in the sugar cane plant.

Sucrose can be removed in usable amounts from a number of plants. Some of them like the sugar cane and sugar beet, produce sugar more abundantly than others and are our main commercial sources. Sugar cane is a giant grass-like plant. It grows in a warm, moist climate and stores its sugar in its long stalk.

At harvest time the sugar cane is cut off near the ground. The long stalks are then stripped of their leaves and chopped into short lengths. The chopped stalks are then shipped to a raw sugar mill. During Rillieux's time the stalks were taken to a mill located on the sugar plantation.

At the mill the stalks are shredded by passing them through crushing rollers. This prepares the stalk fibers for grinding. The shredded cane is next fed through a series of heavy rollers which revolve against each other under great pressure. This action squeezes out the sugar cane juice which is caught in pans below the rollers.

The cane juice is now ready to be changed into raw sugar. It is first treated to remove impurities. Then it is boiled until it thickens and crystals form in it. The boiling evaporates water from the juice. The result is a mixture of molasses and sugar crystals. In a machine called a centrifuge that spins the molasses and sugar around at a high speed, the sugar crystals are separated

from the molasses. Freed from the molasses, the raw
sugar is light brown in color and sticky. Further refining
is necessary to produce the clear, white sugar that you
buy in the store.

At a refinery the raw sugar is dissolved in warm water.
This water-sugar solution is treated a number of times to
remove other impurities and coloring. Now, in order to
have pure sugar crystals, almost all of the water must be
removed or evaporated. And this is where Norbert Rillieux's invention came into the picture. About 1830,
Rillieux began to study the problems of evaporating the
water from the sugar juice so that the sugar would
crystalize.

Up until Rillieux's invention, enormous amounts of
heat were needed to evaporate the water. This required
burning large amounts of fuel which was extremely expensive. Furthermore, much of the heat was wasted in
this very slow process. Rillieux's method of evaporation
involved a new way of using steam heat, which speeded
up sugar production and cut the cost.

FROM NEW ORLEANS TO FRANCE AND BACK

Norbert Rillieux's life was somewhat complicated and
every detail is not known. He was born on a plantation in
New Orleans, Louisiana. Yet, it was in France that he
attended school and spent most of his lifetime.

Rillieux was born in March of 1806. His father, Vincent
Rillieux, a white Frenchman, was an engineer and
master of the plantation on which his mother had been
a black slave. Since Rillieux's birth record indicates

that he was born as a free black, his mother must have been freed from slavery some time before his birth.

At a very young age Norbert Rillieux was recognized as an extremely intelligent child. His father, realizing his ability, sent him to Paris, France, to be educated. This was not unusual for the time, since many black children born to white fathers were sent to Europe for their education. As Norbert went through school he excelled in engineering science. As early as 1830, when only 24 years old, he was an instructor in applied mechanics at L'Ecole Centrale in Paris. By this time too, he had published a series of papers on steam engine work and had several inventions to his name. It was at this time that Rillieux had developed his idea of the multiple-effect evaporator. He tried unsuccessfully to get French machinery manufacturers to build a device to try out his idea.

Rillieux's reputation as a talented engineer somehow reached Louisiana. In New Orleans a new sugar refinery was being built, and the owner of the refinery approached Rillieux and asked him to become his chief engineer. Depressed because he could not get French backing, he decided to try in America. He returned to his homeland in 1830 to accept the job at the sugar refinery.

RILLIEUX'S INVENTION GETS A CHANCE

Rillieux's position as chief engineer of a new sugar factory lasted only a short while. It seems that Vincent Rillieux had a disagreement with the owner of the sugar refinery where his son worked. So Norbert resigned from his position to avoid displeasing his father. There was no chance for Norbert to try his plan on his first job so he decided to set out on his own.

Rillieux's first attempt at using a practical evaporator was in a plantation experiment. He had the help of two friends, but the death of one of them prevented experimenting any further.

Following this first setback, Rillieux went into the real estate business. He hoped to earn enough money to build and operate his own evaporator. He made an enormous fortune but lost it in a bank failure in 1837. Shortly afterwards, however, he made another attempt at operating a triple effect evaporator. This attempt failed too, for reasons that are uncertain, but probably because of mechanical difficulties.

Despite his repeated failures and misfortunes, Rillieux did not quit. Finally, the first of his patents was awarded to him in August, 1843. In the same year he met Theodore Packwood, a sugar manufacturer who owned a sugar plantation near New Orleans. Packwood was interested in Rillieux's invention and invited him to install one on his homestead. In 1845, the "Rillieux system" operated with complete success on Packwood's plantation. Most authorities agree that this was the first workable, multiple-effect vacuum evaporator in the world.

Rillieux's apparatus received quick and loud acclaim. The news of his invention was widespread, and it was recognized as a tremendous contribution to the sugar industry. His evaporating system produced a superior grade of sugar at greatly reduced costs and several factories in Louisiana began using it. The primitive method of evaporating sugar juice in a series of open kettles gave way rapidly not only in Louisiana, but also in Cuba and Mexico. The progressive factory owners of Louisiana were proud of their new methods and many financial reports noted the use of the "Rillieux system."

The years from 1845 to 1855 were years of triumph for Rillieux. His evaporating equipment was a sharp contrast to that of older methods. In the past, slaves used long ladles to transfer boiling sugar juice from one steaming open kettle to another. With Rillieux's discovery, one workman operating a few valves, moved the hot juice in completely enclosed containers. This resulted in savings of labor and steam and prevented the loss of sugar in the process.

Rillieux's system was more than just a change from a hand operation to a mechanical one. It was a complete overthrow of a practice that had changed little through the centuries.

THE RILLIEUX EVAPORATOR—HOW IT WORKED

Rillieux's patent for the evaporator was described as follows:

> A series of vacuum pans, or partial vacuum pans, have been so combined together as to make use of the vapor of the evaporation of the juice in the first, to heat the juice in the second and the vapor from this to heat the juice in the third, which latter is connected with a condenser, the degree of pressure in each successive one being less .... The number of sirup pans may be increased or

decreased at pleasure so long as the last of the series is in conjunction with the condenser.

The evaporator was based on the following idea. Since steam from ordinary water was used for heating sugar juice to evaporate water from it, then the hot vapor (steam) that came from the sugar juice upon evaporation could be used to evaporate another pan of juice. The evaporation started with ordinary steam from heated water and was finished with steam produced from the juice itself.

Below is one of the drawings that accompanied Rillieux's patent. It shows a series of horizontal pans with steam coils. Each pan had the general form of a steam locomotive.

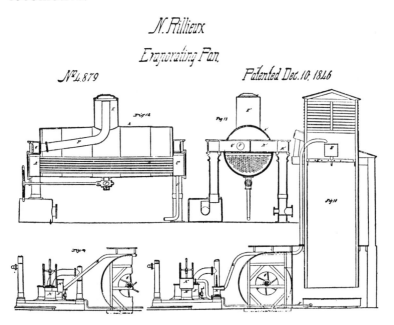

If steam from the first evaporating pan was to be used to heat the juice in the second, and so on, then there had to be a difference in temperature between the heating steam (the vapor) and the boiling temperature of liquid to be heated (the juice). Rillieux solved this problem ingeniously by putting the second and subsequent pans under a vacuum.

As you know, a vacuum or partial vacuum is a space that has few air particles in it. The vacuum lowers the air pressure above the juice. This, in turn, lowers its boiling point. When a liquid reaches its boiling point it evaporates or turns into a gas. In the case of liquid water, the gas is called steam. Water in a pan on your kitchen stove is under normal air pressure and will boil at about 100° C (212°F). However, suppose you carried your pan of water to the top of a high mountain. At great heights the pressure is less because there are fewer air particles in the atmosphere. Since the air pressure is lower the water would change into steam (evaporate) at a temperature less than 100°C.

Sugar juice boils at 90°C under 23 units of vacuum, at 80°C under 40 units of vacuum, and at 70°C under 52 units of vacuum. The higher the vacuum, the lower the boiling point. The vacuums that Rillieux built into his evaporator created a temperature difference between the heating steam and the boiling point of the juice. So by putting those pans which followed the first pan under partial vacuum it became possible to use the steam from the first pan to heat the juice in the second; to use the steam from the second to heat the third pan of juice, etc.

This is what is meant by multiple-effect evaporation.

The advantage of such an arrangement can easily be seen. If one pound of coal yields five pounds of steam in the first pan, these five pounds of steam will evaporate another five pounds of steam. These second five pounds will evaporate still another five pounds and so on. In such a way with four consecutive pans, 20 pounds of water would be evaporated by the initial burning of only one pound of coal.

The key to Rillieux's invention was his thorough understanding of the nature of steam. He managed the repeated use of latent heat. Latent means hidden, not visible or apparent. The steam resulting from the evaporation in the first pan contains practically all of the latent heat of the original steam used to heat the first batch of juice. This was so because liquids absorb heat when they evaporate and become a gas. It was this acquired heat that Rillieux tapped and carried over to the second pan. The latent heat was then used to heat the juice in the second pan. This juice was then able to boil (evaporate) at a lower temperature because of the reduced pressure above the juice caused by the vacuum. At the end of the third evaporating pan there was a condenser that cooled the steam, changing it back into water. Not only did Rillieux's multiple use of latent heat result in the saving of fuel, but the lower evaporating temperatures reduced the risk of the crystallizing sugar becoming discolored from excessive heat.

Before Rillieux, two other inventors had independently developed the vacuum pan and condensing coils. The vacuum pan invented in 1813 was modified by Rillieux. DeGrand, a French inventor, built an evaporator that condensed the steam from the vacuum pan using cool sugar juice. However, DeGrand's system did not properly use the latent heat of the vapors. It remained for Norbert Rillieux to modify what had been tried before him, putting some old and new ideas together into a successful combination.

RILLIEUX RETURNS TO FRANCE

Sometime after 1855, Norbert Rillieux left Louisiana and returned to France. Some believe that he did not want to leave and probably did so because of the prejudice and discrimination faced by black Americans. Rillieux's professional status was solid. He was one of the most sought after engineers in Louisiana. However, although his ideas, ability, and achievements were accepted, Rillieux as a person was not treated fairly because of his racial ancestry.

When Rillieux was employed on various sugar plantations as a consulting engineer, the "color problem" was met by providing him special living quarters. Because of his "colored" blood, he could not be entertained in the plantation owner's home, or in the house of any other white person. Although there are not personal records of his being unjustly treated in America, his secretary in France, noted that he battled against prejudice for thirteen years before he could erect his first multiple-effect evaporator.

In this country during the 1850's, free black people were more and more restrained. Although they never reached the very low status of slaves, free blacks like Rillieux were subjected to restrictions and ridicule. By 1855 they could not walk the streets of New Orleans without permission. A traveling black person could not stop off in New Orleans unless represented by a white person. It is quite probable that the social conditions faced by black people during the pre-Civil War days made Rillieux decide to return to France.

Not only was Rillieux's social status lowered because of his color, but at least one of his engineering achievements was probably ignored because of his race. He worked out a practical plan for a sewerage system for the city of New Orleans but local authorities at the time refused to accept and adopt it. Many people believe that Rillieux's plan was never accepted because of the prejudice that existed at that time.

Curiously, it was back in France, where there was little racial discrimination that Rillieux faced even more trouble with his inventions and patents. It seems that a German who had worked for the firm in Philadelphia that constructed Rillieux's first multiple-effect evaporator, had copied the plans and brought them back to a factory in Germany. From these stolen designs, the first evaporator in France had been installed in a sugar beet factory in 1852. Due to a complete misunderstanding of Rillieux's designs, this evaporator and others constructed like it in Europe operated very poorly. The engineers who tried to use Rillieux's designs apparently lacked the scientific knowledge that Rillieux had when he first built his evaporators in America. So when Rillieux reached France in the late 1850's, he had a bad name among French sugar engineers. He could find no Europeans who were interested in trying his sugar refining process.

Completely discouraged, he lost all interest in sugar engineering and machinery. He turned to archaeology and spent ten years in this profession. In 1880, a leading sugar planter from New Orleans visited Paris and was surprised to find Rillieux at work translating Egyptian writing in a library.

And then, for some unknown reason, at the age of 75, Rillieux renewed his interest in his evaporator. So he sought to obtain a patent for his system of manufacturing sugar from the sugar beet plant, and was finally successful in 1881. The French sugar beet houses accepted Rillieux's efforts and he received full credit for halving the fuel costs they were presently expending. Yet, the experts were still not willing to recognize that the multiple-effect evaporating process was created by Rillieux way back in the 1830's, and that it had worked. Again, he retired from the work to which he had contributed so much. Even at the time of his death in 1894, he was still active and alert. According to Rillieux's best friend, "He died more from a broken heart than from the weight of years."

Through time Norbert Rillieux's place in America's history of industrial science and technology was lost. If they mention him at all, very few of the historical sources mention the fact that he was a black man. In fact, in the general biographical histories of American inventors, Rillieux is completely ignored.

In 1914, a Dutch sugar expert published a paper on evaporation. He was impressed by Rillieux's work in the field and started a movement toward giving worldwide recognition to him. He gathered together other authorities in the sugar processing industry, including the President of the International Society of Sugar Cane Technologists. Together they contacted the sugar interests throughout the world for contributions. The response was almost unanimous in support of the recognition due Rillieux even though a few beet sugar scientists in Germany would still not accept the claim that Rillieux was the true inventor of multiple-effect evaporation. There were, however, thirty-eight contributors to the memorial, representing practically every cane and sugar beet producing country in the world.

If you ever visit the Louisiana State Museum in New Orleans you will see a bronze plaque from the sugar industry. The plaque has a relief bust of Rillieux. Its inscription reads:

To honor and commemorate
Norbert Rillieux
Born at New Orleans, La., March 18, 1806
and died at Paris, France
October 8, 1894.
Inventor of Multiple Evaporation and its
Application into the Sugar Industry
This tablet was dedicated in 1934 by
Corporations representing the
Sugar Industry all over the world.

GRANVILLE T. WOODS

1856-1910

The "Black Edison"

On January 14, 1886, the *Catholic Tribune* (Cincinnati, Ohio) said:

"Granville T. Woods, the greatest colored inventor in the history of the race, and equal, if not superior to any inventor in the country, is destined to revolutionize the mode of street car transit. The results of his experiments are no longer a question of doubt. He has excelled in every possible way in all his inventions. He is master of the situation, and his name will be handed down to coming generations as one of the greatest inventors of his time. He has not only elevated himself to the hightest position among inventors, but has shown beyond doubt the possibility of a colored man inventing as well as one of any other race."

About a year later, in April of 1887, the same paper said:

"Mr. Woods who is the greatest electrician in the world, still continues to add to his long list of electrical inventions.

The latest device he invented is the Synchronous Multiplex Railway Telegraph. By means of this system, the railway dispatcher can note the position of any train on the route at a glance. The system also provides means for telegraphing to and from the train while in motion. . . . In using the devices there is no possibility of collision between trains, as each train can always be informed of the position of the other while in motion. . . ."

Earlier, in 1887, the Cincinnati Colored Citizen, in its January 29th issue said:

"We take great pleasure in congratulating Mr. G.T. Woods on his success in becoming so prominent that his skill and knowledge of his chosen art compare with that of any one of our best electricians of the day."

At the time these articles appeared, the Woods' Railway Telegraph Company was located in Cincinnati, Ohio. These rather generous tributes show how proud Cincinnati citizens were of one of their own. But they also reflected the real electro-mechanical genius of Granville Woods. During his lifetime he was awarded some 50 patents for his various inventions. Most of these were devices that had to do with the control and distribution of electricity. However, Woods was a versatile man and some of his patents were in non-electrical fields as well.

More than a dozen inventions by Woods improved the electric railways. They included an electro-mechanical brake, tunnel construction for an electric railway, and an electric railway conduit. In 1892, hundreds of children who visited the famous Coney Island amusement park in New York rode on a miniature electric railway that Woods invented. The small train was something very new. It had no exposed wires and required no secondary batteries. The electric current used to run the trains was taken from iron blocks placed at intervals of 12 feet between the rails. By an ingenious arrangement of magnets and switches, the current was turned on only at those blocks passed over by the moving cars.

In addition to his electric railway works, Woods had many other electrical inventions to his credit. They included improvements in telegraphy, telephone instruments, a phonograph, an automatic cut-off for electric circuits and a regulator for electric motors.

Perhaps Woods' most noteworthy electrical inventions was his Induction Telegraphy. This system was designed to send telegraphic messages to and from a moving train. This was important in the 1800's because it could help prevent collisions between trains by keeping each train informed of the whereabouts of the one immediately ahead or following it

How did Granville Woods come to be the electrical genius that he was?

LEARNING BY DOING

Woods was born in Columbus, Ohio, in 1865. He attended school there until he was 10 years old. At this young age he began working in a machine shop that repaired railroad equipment. It was here that his lifelong interest in railroads started.

As a boy, Woods was always anxious to learn. The mysteries of electricity intrigued him and he read every book he could find on the subject. From each department in the machine shop where he worked he tried to learn as much as he could about electrical engineering. With part of his weekly earnings he paid for private instruction from the master mechanic at the shop. His basic mechanical and electrical knowledge was increased by many other jobs he held and what he learned at one job helped him to get and work at another.

In 1872, when he was sixteen years old, Granville Woods headed West. After some difficulty in getting a job he finally obtained one as a fireman and later as an engineer on one of the Iron Mountain Railroads in Missouri. While he was working for this railroad company he had plenty of leisure time and he spent all of it studying and experimenting with electricity.

Shortly afterwards, Woods moved on to Springfield, Illinois. Here he became employed at a rolling mill where iron and steel was rolled into plates and bars. When he was twenty, Woods left Illinois and headed East to attend a technical school. For two years he received training in electrical and mechanical engineering. Even while attending school he worked a six and a half day week. His days were spent in a machine shop. During the late afternoons and evenings he attended classes.

In 1878, after completing his two-year course, Woods went to sea as an engineer aboard the *Ironsides*, a British steamer. He was able to visit nearly every continent in the world. After two years he went back to railroads—this time handling a steam locomotive for a railroad company in Cincinnati.

During his past years of travel and study, Woods had often been denied work because he was a black man. But he never let this situation depress him for long. However, despite his studies and hard work, racial prejudice held him back. Even with his experience and training his blackness prevented him from advancing in the engineering jobs that he had held. So he finally decided to open his own shop to work on and sell the inventions he had in mind.

BECOMING A "BLACK EDISON"

Because of his many successful electrical inventions, Woods can be compared to the inventor Thomas Edison and has been called by some people—the "Black Edison."

In the early stages of his career he organized the Woods Electric Company in Cincinnati. This firm took over many of his early patents, and from 1884 on, his inventions began to multiply in number and value each year. As his reputation in the electrical-engineering world grew, he found that some of the largest and most prosperous corporations in the United States were interested in his work, General Electric, Westinghouse, American Bell Telephone and American Engineering.

Bell Telephone purchased an apparatus for transmitting messages by electricity. Here is how he described this invention: (Patent No. 315,368—April 7, 1885)

"In the ordinary mode of sending telegraphic messages the operator uses a "finger-key" whose duties are to irregularly make and break the circuit or to vary the tension of the electric current traversing the 'line wire', the 'key' being operated by the varying pressure of the operator's finger. This key as ordinarily constructed cannot be operated in any other way or for any other purpose than just mentioned. The message thus transmitted is received by an instrument known as a 'receiver' or 'sounder', which causes audible atmospheric vibrations in response to the pulsations of the electric current traversing the line-wire.

It is well known that both the sender and the recipient of messages thus transmitted must be skilled operators. It is also well known that such sounder as usually constructed will not respond to very weak electric currents, such as used in telephony. My system (called by me 'Telegraphony') entirely overcomes the failings of the ordinary key and sounder and has a wide range of usefulness, it being capable of use by inexperienced persons, for if, for example, the operator cannot read or write the Morse signals, he has only (by means of a suitable switch) to 'cut' the battery out of the main-line circuit and 'cut' it into a local circuit and then speak near the key. This having been done, the sounder at the receiving station will cause the air to vibrate in unison with the electric pulsations that traverse the line-wire. The person at the receiving-station will thus receive the message as articulate speech."

Another of Woods' remarkable inventions was a device for regulating electric motors. In an electric motor, electrical energy is changed into energy of motion or mechanical energy. Many of the machines in your home such as a vacuum cleaner, a washing machine, and a food mixer are run by electric motors. When using electrical power it is necessary at times to change the speed of the rotating shaft of a motor without changing or disturbing the electrical voltage at its source. Up until Woods' invention, changing the speed of the shaft was done by adding coils of electrically resistant wire to the motors. These coils called *resistances*, would drain off some of the electricity coming into the motor. But they became hot very quickly like electric coils in a bread toaster, and using them was really a waste of electricity. Woods, by using a complicated device called a dynamotor, was able to reduce the size of the resistances. This lessened the large losses of electricity and the chances of over-heating.

Certain parts of his motor regulator were challenged by rival inventors. And in 1895 hearings were held at the United States Patent Office to establish the true inventor. As it turned out, only one of the rival inventors had his invention even partly completed. The Patent Office investigation proved that Woods had obviously developed his invention first because there was no other prior model for him to follow or copy. In fact, when Woods completed his model, the other inventors were just beginning theirs. And it was much later before they eventually developed similar devices.

Through his business activities and patent defenses, Woods became quite knowledgeable about the legal aspects regarding inventions. His electric motor regulator was not the only invention he had to defend. His most famous invention, the Induction Telegraph, a system for communicating to and from moving trains, was also contested by a rival inventor who had been working on a similar system.

PREVENTING TRAIN COLLISIONS

During the 1800's, newspapers were filled with reports of collisions between railway trains in all sections of the country. Frequently a train would run into the one ahead of it on the track. Some way of warning an approaching train had to be found. Many methods of signaling between moving trains and stations had been tried. None were foolproof. Many engineers believed that a solution could be found in the field of electrical science, since electricity could be used to send messages along wires.

Because electricity moves very rapidly in a conducting wire, these impulses are received almost at the same time they are sent. Telegraphy was the first method used to send messages by electricity. Telegraphy is a Greek word meaning "to write at a distance," i.e. to send news by signals to distant places. The first telegraph system was invented by Samuel Morse in 1837.

The simplest telegraph system consists of a battery (for a supply of electricity) wires for conducting electricity, a key, and a sounder. The key is a special piece of apparatus for sending messages (electrical impulses) and the sounder is a piece of equipment which receives the messages. These are sent by tapping out words, letter by letter, with the telegraph key. The letters are received at the other end as a "click" or "buzz" sound. Using a code (the International Morse Code) the duration of the sounds (long and short) can be translated into letters making up the words of the message.

The use of telegraphy had helped to reduce the number of train accidents. The various types of telegraphic equipment required human operators—one on the train and one at the train station. Telegraph messages between the two operators kept each informed about the location of the trains on the track. Even so, there were still accidents. During heavy fog, the signalman at the station could hardly see beyond his range of sight. And the railway signalmen, being human, were capable of error. At night, a lone signalman at a station could easily become drowsy and fall asleep. A system was still needed that would not have to rely solely on one telegraph man at the station.

The improvement of electric telegraphy made possible what was called the "Block System." The railways were divided into blocks or sections. A train could not leave one block and enter the next until it received an "all clear" message over the telegraph line. This system was used in special sections of the track such as long tunnels. Although the "Block System" had a good record of preventing accidents—some serious collisions still occurred, for sometimes the automatic signals failed to work. When this happened a station telegraph operator would often become flustered and send out unclear messages over the telegraph. This mixup would often result in two trains colliding in the same block.

There was another more basic problem with train telegraphic equipment. Any telegraph setup required a continuous wire connection between the key and the sounder. Thus, some part of the moving trains had to be in direct contact with the conducting wire between the telegraph equipment in the station and that on the train. Only under favorable conditions did the best of these train telegraphic systems work. Many times the messages were incomplete or interrupted because the metal contact between the moving train and the conducting wire was poor.

Granville Woods came forth with a system of train telegraph signaling that did not depend on contact between some part of the moving train and the conducting wire to the station. He designed a system that used the principle of electrical induction—hence the naming of his invention as the Induction Telegraph System.

Before looking at the invention let's understand the principle of electrical induction.

Suppose you had a length of wire that was conducting electricity. Let's call it the primary wire. Now suppose you placed another length of wire like the first, parallel and close to, but not touching, the primary wire. The electric current in the primary wire could cause or induce electricity to flow into the second wire.

Induction telegraphy was not discovered by Woods,

but it was his idea to use it in a railroad telegraph system. What Woods did was to lay an electric wire between the rails. Each end of this ground wire was connected to a battery and a telegraph key and sounder at the station. In one of the cars on the train there was also a battery, key, and sounder. Underneath the car containing this equipment was suspended an electric cable. It ran the length of the car and was connected only to the telegraph equipment inside the car. This cable was eight to ten inches above and parallel to the wire that ran along the ground between the rails.

When messages, as impulses of electricity, were sent into the cable suspended from the car, an electric current was induced into that portion of the ground wire directly under the moving car. The strength of the induced current was strong enough so that it could be picked up by the receiving apparatus at the station. In the same way, electrical impulses generated at a train station and passed into the ground wire were picked up by the cable attached to the train as it moved over the ground wire. No metallic connection or direct contact was needed between the moving train and the station telegraph equipment. A train either in motion or at rest, could receive a message from a station in back of or in front of it. And likewise, a moving or resting train could send a message to a station.

In his letter of application for a patent on his Induction Telegraph System, Granville Woods described his invention in this way:

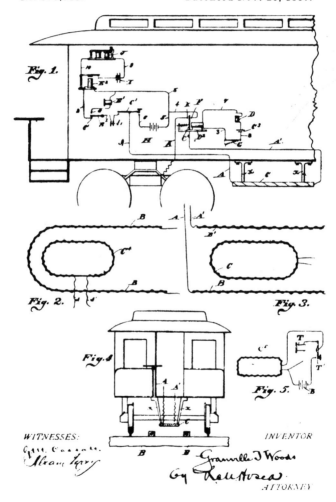

G. T. WOODS.
INDUCTION TELEGRAPH SYSTEM.
No. 373,915.   Patented Nov. 29, 1887.

Granville Wood's patent for his Railway Induction Telegraph System made travel by rail much safer, for it helped to eliminate many train collisions.

To all whom it may concern:

Be it known that I, Granville T. Woods, a citizen of the United States residing at Cincinnati, Ohio, have invented new and useful Improvements in Induction-Telegraph Systems, of which the following is a specification.

My invention relates to systems of electric communication between two moving railway trains or vehicles, or between the same and a fixed station or stations, and transmits the signals to and from the vehicle by means of induction, whereby an electric impulse upon the line-conductor is caused to produce a corresponding impulse upon the similarly arranged conductor carried by the vehicle in close proximity to the line-conductor. . .

Any code of signals may be employed in my system of communication. A telephone-receiver and a telegraph-relay may be arranged so that either one may cut into the helical circuit when a signal is to be received. . . .

Granville Woods' patent for his Railway Induction Telegraph System was not easily won. Another inventor who had been working on a similar telegraph system for moving trains challenged Woods' patent. In two Patent Office cases of Woods vs Phelps, Woods was declared the inventor.

In completing and patenting upward of 50 different inventions, Woods appears to have surpassed in his time every other black inventor in the number and variety of his inventions. This record lasted for over a quarter of a century without interruption until Woods passed away in New York in January of 1910.

In 1917, an article entitled "The Negro in the Field of Invention" appeared in the *Journal of Negro History*. It was written by Henry E. Baker, a black man and an assistant examiner at the United States Patent Office in Washington D.C. He said in his article:

So far as the writer is aware there is no inventor of the colored race whose creative genius has covered quite so wide a field as that of Granville T. Woods, nor one whose achievements have attracted more universal attention and favorable comment from technical and scientific journals both in this country and abroad.

EPILOGUE

The stories of the individual black Americans in this book are American stories. Each inventor presented here is an example of the human creativity, aspirations, and struggles that have shaped our country. Each man, in his own way, contributed to the industrial, techno- logical, and economic development of America. They were a part of its making. And, when all Americans, young and old, black and white, come to know these men, we will all have a greater understanding and respect for America and for all of its people.

Robert C. Hayden

ACKNOWLEDGEMENTS

Illustrations and quotations are reproduced courtesy of the following institutions:

page 16:   Johnson Publishing Company

page 20:   Addison-Wesley Publishing Company, from a miscellaneous advertising brochure, provided by Mr. Garrett A. Morgan, Jr., Euclid, Ohio

page 24:   Johnson Publishing Company

pages 26, 27:   Addison-Wesley Publishing Company, from a miscellaneous advertising brochure, provided by Mr. Garrett A. Morgan, Jr., Euclid, Ohio

pages 28, 29:   courtesy of Mrs. Karen Morgan Haithcox, Cleveland, Ohio

page 30:   courtesy of Mr. Dudley Onley, New Bedford, Massachusetts

page 38:   The Whaling Museum, New Bedford, Massachusetts

page 44:   Johnson Publishing Company
pages 49, 53:   courtesy of Mrs. Frederick Jones from Minnesota
                  Historical Society
page 56:   Boston Public Library
page 60:   courtesy of United Shoe Machinery Corporation
page 73:   Boston Public Library
page 78:   New York Public Library
pages 86, 90,   courtesy of The Latimer Collection, Miss
       91:        Winifred L. Norman
page 92:   New York Public Library
pages 95, 100:   Boston Public Library
page 104:   New York Public Library
page 113:   Boston Public Library
page 120:   Johnson Publishing Company
page 132:   Boston Public Library

INDEX

Anderson, Jo, 9

Beard, Thomas, 62, 65
Bell, Alexander Graham, 80, 84
"Black Edison," 15, 121, 125
Black inventors, (list of), 13–14
Black, Jeremiah S., 9
Blair, Henry, 10–11
"Block System," 129–130

Carbon filament, 85–87
    illus., 86
Civil War, 8, 10, 14–15

Consolidated Lasting
    Machine Co., 74–75, 77
Cotton gin, 7–8

Edison Pioneers, 80, 88–89
Edison, Thomas, 80, 85, 88–89
Eskimo, 40–41

Forten, James, 10
France, 110, 116–118

G. A. Morgan Hair Refining
    Co., 24

ABOUT THE AUTHOR

Robert C. Hayden has been associated with science and science writing throughout his professional career. EIGHT BLACK AMERICAN INVENTORS takes its place alongside his SEVEN BLACK AMERICAN SCIENTISTS as another notable contribution to the American scene. Mr. Hayden, his wife, and their four children reside in Newton, Massachusetts. He is Executive Director of the Metropolitan Council for Educational Opportunity (METCO) in Boston, Massachusetts.